QUESTIONS FOR VISIONARY LEADERS

Visionary Coaching Guide

Mihail Bogdan

Copyright © 2020 Mihail Bogdan

All rights reserved.

No part of this book may be reproduced, or stored in a retrieval system, or transmitted in any form or by any means, electronic, mechanical, photocopying, recording, or otherwise, without express written permission of the publisher.

ISBN: 9798633349047

Cover design by: Simeon Bogdan

To Ema, Timotei and Sara. You are all a great blessing to me and to many others.

To the family I come from. I appreciate your bold thinking and pioneering spirit.

To my colleagues from Youth With A Mission. Our value number five inspired me to write this book.

To all those who dare to dream and act full of hope for the promising future. Thanks to you, the world will be a better place for all.

If I had an hour to solve a problem and my life depended on the solution, I would spend the first 55 minutes determining the proper question to ask... for once I know the proper question, I could solve the problem in less than five minutes.

ALBERT EINSTEIN

CONTENTS

Title Page	1
Copyright	2
Dedication	3
Epigraph	4
Foreword	11
Preface	15
Introduction	21
How to Use the Book?	25
PART I - PRIOR TO IMPLEMENTATION	29
1. Personal Identity	31
1.1. What Defines Your Identity?	33
1.2. Scenarios for Reflection and Awareness	35
1.3. Values, Principles, Priorities, and Qualities	38
1.4. Talents and Skills	40
1.5. Inspiration, Challenges, and Development	41
1.6. Lifestyle	47
2. Questions for Different Types of Personality	51
2.1. Myers Briggs	
2.2. DISC	
2.3. Enneagram	
3. Visionary Leader	85

3.1. Awareness and Positioning	86
3.2. Visionary Mentality	88
3.3. Leadership Styles	94
4. Exploring the Society	99
4.1. 10 Areas of Society	101
4.2. Thinking Rich and Altruistic [1]	122
4.3. Understanding the Needs[2]	
4.4. Challenging the Status-Quo[3]	127
4.5. Capitalizing on Trends[4]	129
4.5. Connecting Opportunities[5]	131
5. Vision	133
5.1. Vision, Mission, Strategy, and Values	134
5.2. Impressions From the Future	136
5.3. Communicating the Vision	142
6. Common identity	145
6.1. Values	147
6.2. Guidelines	149
6.3. Brand	150
7. Mission	151
7.1. The Meaning of the Mission	152
7.2. The Purpose of the Mission	154
7.3. The Elaboration of the Mission Statement	155
7.4. Communicating the Mission	156
PART II - FOR IMPLEMENTATION	159
8. Strategy	161
8.1. Planning the Journey to Your Destination	163
8.2. Strategic Priorities	165
8.3. Objectives, Goals and Tactical Actions	168

8.4. Stages and Deadlines	172
8.5. Tests: Perseverance and Results	174
9. The Team	177
9.1. People and Roles	178
9.2. The Ethos of the Team	182
9.3. Working atmosphere	183
9.4. Networking	185
9.5. Leadership, Development, and Care[32]	
10. Capital and Resources	191
10.1. Perspectives That Make a Difference	193
10.2. The Strengths of the Organization	195
10.3. Material Resources	198
10.4. Time Management	202
Appendix 1. Cultivating Multiplication	203
Bibliography	205
About The Author	209

FOREWORD

I met Mihail a couple of years ago when he participated in the "Foundational Coaching Skills Training" in order to learn coaching. It was evident that he was passionate to develop himself as well as integrate the coaching approach in his context, work, and leadership.

In his book, Mihail emphasizes that before we can create hope for the world we live in, we need to personally and corporately reflect, through questions and dialogue. Then can we discover and implement solutions that bring about the change we hope for in the midst of the challenges we face.

His book is a treasure chest filled with questions (drawn from various models) that will help us get started or to deepen our search for insights and solutions, both for our personal development as well as our corporate responsibility in society. The depth of knowing and being who we are, determines how we live. Who I am is how I live. Who I am is how I lead or coach. We are often unaware that we hold false assumptions, have limited perspectives or judgments that limit our choices and sometimes lead to destructive consequences. Asking questions and creating meaningful dialogue before we act, empowers us to deepen our awareness and insight, so we can make the changes where it matters most: from the inside out, from our changed perspectives to our daily actions. One small step at a time. Our change impacts others, who impact their family, their group,

their team, their organization, their community, their city, their nation, by being who they are meant to be. Our decisions matter for the kind of society and world we and our children will live in.

Enjoy and benefit from the power and beauty of the questions in this book and add your own. Those around you will be enriched by what you discover. Albert Einstein had a wonderful approach: "If I had an hour to solve a problem and my life depended on the solution, I would spend the first 55 minutes determining the proper question to ask... for once I know the proper question, I could solve the problem in less than five minutes." Let us start with asking the proper questions, so we can find the the answers our society needs.

Wolfgang G. Jani
Professional Coach & Coach Trainer
Budapest, Hungary

PREFACE

Interacting with people with different types of personalities, I realized that some are more likely to be concerned about the future than others; some people seem to live in the future only, while others live in the moment. Some seem to always see possibilities and opportunities, while others can only acknowledge the reality, what already exists.

Studying and comparing personality types, I discovered that some people naturally tend to not see the forest for the trees, while others see it the opposite way.

From my work experience, one on one and with teams, I noticed that many people pay attention to specific details, while some are more interested in the bigger picture, but without any real commitment to achieve something. Some are more theoretical, others are more pragmatic. Some are more innovative, others are more practical. Some look for hidden meanings, others look for the concrete value.

Rarely have I met leaders who manage to be concerned about the future, conceptual and innovative, with a good overview, but who also value the present moment, the tangible, the practical actions and the details that make the difference.

Inborn potential is worth exploring and exploiting, as well as the ability to operate in complementary aspects. This is how the idea of this visionary coaching guide was born: To maximize what comes naturally, your strengths, but also to be more

intentional outside the comfort zone. That same potential should also be maximized within teams, and society in general; just as every human being in his unique way is important and valuable, together we complement one another and can work together to make the world a better place.

Some people are just a question away from a new revelation, an open door away from unique opportunities, a quick exit from ignorance, from the ordinary, from loss, from failures, etc.

Before writing this question book, my own experience helped me enormously, but so did a formal training in three areas related to the subject of this book: pioneering, leadership, and life coaching.

The vision of the book. The following scenario is what stimulated me to write this guide: *visionaries at the beginning of (a new) adventure, starting and traveling enthusiastically to their target destination, while they are delighted to use the (intellectual) fuel offered by me. This fuel is already very useful to other coaches and leaders who are passionate about guiding others to success.*

The mission of the book. The essential contribution of this guide should be the following: *to stimulate the creative potential of leaders in order to fulfill their mission with skill and satisfaction.*

I hope this guide will be very useful to you, especially if you are one of the three types of people:
- An inborn visionary, innovative thinker, someone who acts strategically for a wonderful future;
- A leader of the future or of today, who intentionally aims high;
- A coach who believes in both, to empower them for

change and success.

I strongly believe that this guide will be helpful, not just for individual processing, but also for leadership teams, organizations, small and medium-sized businesses, corporations, multinationals, governmental and international institutions at the the highest level.

INTRODUCTION

A true leader is a visionary, and a true visionary is a leader. Unlike a dreamer, the visionary is a pioneer, concerned with the present and the future, with actions, with implementation and with significant achievements. A visionary is not just an activist, just for the sake of action; he is also concerned with the meaning of things, with his own identity and his purpose, with the society he lives in, with its progress and the well-being of other people.

Book Structure

The structure of the book contains two main parts:

I. **Who, why, by whom, by what** – prior the implementation of your vision (the first seven chapters).
II. **How, with whom, with what, when** – close to the implementation process (the last three chapters).
At the same time, the book follows a natural course from focusing on the visionary leader, towards what he will develop and lead: movements, organizations, businesses or institutions.

Content

The book is a Visionary Coaching Guide, with over 2400

questions structured by sections, categories and subcategories. Some questions are more general than others.

Some questions are excellent for personal evaluation, others are useful for brainstorming in small groups; especially the second part: the implementation of your vision contains questions which can be very relevant for different management structures and decision-makers.

The main sections contain questions focused on the following:

1. Personal identity and development: qualities and principles, role models and guides, motivation and devotion, spirituality and creativity.
2. Personality types: Myers-Brigg, DISC and Enneagram indicators.
3. Visionary leader: mindset, and leadership styles.
4. Exploring the society: areas of our society, needs, status quo, trends, and opportunities.
5. The leader's vision: stake, importance, relevance, story, research, target group, and vision statement.
6. Common identity: values and common specification, brand.
7. Common mission: key actions, responsibilities, impact, and mission statement.
8. Strategies and Tactics: priorities, goals, purposes, risks, stages, and deadlines.
9. Team dynamics: people and key roles, working environment, networking, multiplication, progress.
10. Capital and resources: abilities, assets, opportunities, innovation, investments, and management.

HOW TO USE THE BOOK?

This book is not necessarily one that you want to read from the beginning to the end, until you finish it.
It is rather a guide with coaching questions which can help you in a specific situation, whether what you are facing is in your personal life or in leadership.

Out of the more than 2400 questions, try stopping at one; take time to reflect alone or with a group. You can use supporting questions in a specific section of a certain chapter. Or you can go entirely through one of the ten chapters.

In addition, the book can also be used for self-coaching, a resource that you can constantly reach to, from designing a dream to achieving it.

You can jump directly to questions about exploring a dream, how to accomplish a bold vision, or how to achieve a certain goal.

This guide is also useful for leaders who want to be stimulated in asking the right questions of people who are visionaries, or those who want to think and act more idealistically, more strategically and more purposefully.

At some point you may want to focus on useful questions in exploring new horizons. Other times you can examine the process

of accomplishing your vision. At some other time you can focus on how to progress with the implementation. Sometimes, you will simply want to enjoy stimulating your thinking with these theoretical and useful questions.

PART I - PRIOR TO IMPLEMENTATION

Personal Identity, Personality Types, Visionary Leader, Society, Vision, Common Identity, Common Mission

1. PERSONAL IDENTITY

who are you before leading?

1.1. WHAT DEFINES YOUR IDENTITY?

What are your strengths, which ones, in the face of failure, would still not affect your self-esteem? What about those strengths if threatened, would they affect your self-esteem?

How confident are you about your identity under risks and pressure?

How well do you manage to cope with the temptation of manipulating other people to get what you want?

How much do you struggle to get noticed?

If visionaries are creators who create something that doesn't exist, who is your role model creator?

How convinced are you that divinity has a special calling for you? To what extent did you get to know your calling? Are you practicing it at the moment?

If people had to choose between believing in you or in your vision, what would you like them to choose?

What are your strengths, which might motivate those who know you to give you more confidence?

Which circumstances would be the best for people to get to

know you and trust you more?

What gives you authority in the field in which you are working?

To what extent are you willing to engage others in accomplishing the vision you wish to achieve?

How do you see your calling connected to something superior to you, to divinity?

What is your fundamental source for importance and value?

How important and valuable is your source?

What is the highest expression of who you really are?

1.2. SCENARIOS FOR REFLECTION AND AWARENESS

In The Face Of Changes:

You are a member of a leading team of an international organization. A sudden change of the management structure is proposed, which also affects the purpose and role of your position.

What are the things that you think would be important to clarify before you take a stand?

What are the factors that will influence your pro or con argument?

What other more profound factors could there be?

How much does the motivation behind the change matter? What about the long-term impact? What about the person proposing the change?

How likely is it for you to be the initiator of change? Or for the others to not share your opinions?

What is distinctive about how you would act in such a situation?

In The Face Of Opportunities:

> *In your field of interest, if you had the opportunity to lay the foundations of a prestigious local institution or an international movement, what would you choose?*

What is the most important to you?

How would your team discuss this matter?

> *What would you choose between the opportunity to fund an online business that generates a profit with minimal involvement from you, or an NGO that saves several communities from poverty?*

For what reason would you choose the first option? What about the second?

How much does the profit matter when compared to a noble cause with significant results?

In The Face Of Challenges:

> *In your favorite field, you would have to decide whether to take the lead of a well-known international organization that has been downgraded in recent years, or to fund a new one from scratch, with minimal support.*

What are the factors that matter to you in making this decision?

What are the opportunities you see in both options? What

about the risks?

How much does it matter to you to try a certain option, despite any criticism?

1.3. VALUES, PRINCIPLES, PRIORITIES, AND QUALITIES

Values

What are your personal values? In what order?

How important is it to be surrounded by people who meet high standards?

How important is it for you to be connected to the divinity, to the values and desires of God?

Principles

What are your principles regarding: work? What about the team? What about the money? What about relationships?

If you were to find out about any unethical or illegal activities, would you consider making yourself a complicit by keeping the secret?

How would you react in the face of an opportunity that would put you in a conflict of interest?

Priorities

What are your priorities, considering: quality and quantity, character and performance, purpose and means, etc.

Personal Qualities In Different Circumstances

Do you feel at ease when you confront others when it is necessary? What about creating a positive work environment in which mistakes are tolerated?

How natural does it feel to accept negative feedback?

How likely are you to react in favor of your people to face injustice? What about in favor of others? What if you were to lose?

What would hold you back from telling the truth when it should be spoken?

If you were to confront someone, would you be able to tell them the truth in a way they would be receptive?

For what reasons would you like people to join your vision?

What is your tendency, as a leader, between forcing those you lead to do things well or to have your own job done well?

1.4. TALENTS AND SKILLS

Innate Talents

What are the talents you think you've been endowed with in your DNA?

What special capabilities do you think you were born with?

What actions feel more natural than others? Why?

How could you develop innate talents more?

What would make them flourish? In what circumstances?

How do you perceive the potential of your innate talents?

Developed Skills

What are the skills you have developed better than most people?

What skills have you been particularly appreciated for?

What is the thing you have become more confident doing?

If you were to make a list of 10 of your skills, what would the first three be? What circumstances would point them out? How could you maximize their potential?

1.5. INSPIRATION, CHALLENGES, AND DEVELOPMENT

Role Models And Standards

What are the three most important features of people you would like to spend your spare time with? In what order? What about a brainstorming meeting on a strategic decision?

As a visionary, what are your sources of inspiration?

If you had the chance to spend an hour with any three contemporary people, one on one, who would you choose? For what? What about if they were from your town? What about if they were historical characters?

What are the top three visionaries in your city that come to your mind right now?

What three visionaries do you know in person?

Who are the first three visionaries you appreciate or admire?

Who inspired you the most in your main projects so far?

What about for your main vision at this point in time?

As a visionary leader, what are the things that lift you up? Particularly...?

What are the things that are holding you back? The first one being…?

What do you think is the biggest temptation for a visionary? What about a huge risk? What would it be for you?

Personal Development

How do you manage your freedom of development? By what values and principles? Through what specific actions?

What are your arguments for personal development? If you would summarize them to only one, what would it say?

How do you think personal development influences your passion and vision? What about the other way around?

What are the areas in which you have progressed the most so far? What about the ones you fell behind?

In what areas do you think you can excel?

What are the areas in which you think it would be important for you to progress? In what order?

What are the specific aspects you want to develop as a priority?

In what ways would you say you have progressed so far?

What is your favorite way of personal development?

What would be the ideal environment for your personal development?

Who are the people who have contributed the most to your development?

In what ways are you connected to certain environments that facilitate personal development?

How much time do you allot weekly for personal development? What about monthly? Or annually?

How much time would you like to spend for personal development?

How much time will you spend for personal development?

How motivated are you to do this?

What is standing in the way of your personal development?

Which things (good or bad) would you give up in favor of personal development?

Spirituality And Creativity

Spirituality

What does "spirituality" mean to you?

What role does spirituality play in your life?

How does divinity inspire you?

How much do you think God is in your favor, wanting you to prosper?

How much do you consider yourself blessed by divinity to truly think and act in a wealthy manner? How empowered do you consider yourself?

What are the generally valid principles for prosperity? How do you know you know?

How connected do you feel with the divinity?

How much do you feel like you are in a partnership with God regarding your vision and your plans?

Practical Spirituality

Why is spirituality important to you?

When was the last time you felt like the excellent idea that came to you, seemed to have a divine origin?

How much of your time would you like to invest in reflecting, meditating and communicating with God?

What does it mean to you to spend quality time with God?

What should happen to experience this more often?

How would this reflect in your schedule? How often?

How could you practice your spirituality solely for the good of others? How could you be more practical?

The Source Of The Creator Genius - Theoretical And Philosophical Reflections[1]

How do innovators get to their ideas?

When does the enlightenment occur? What favors the appearance of the revelations?

What role does divinity have or can have in resourcefulness and creativity?

Is creativity innate to human beings?

Does the result of human creativity have any moral dimension?

What are the most likely sources of wisdom? Do you consider any one of them to be of a divine nature?

What is the process of generating brilliant, creative ideas?

What is the source of brilliant talent?

How human is creativity in its essence and origin? Does it belong exclusively to human beings? If so, when did it emerge, and how? If not, does anybody else have it, and in what way is it different from the one humans have?

What is the difference between making and creating?

Do you believe there is a correlation between ability, wisdom human resourcefulness and grace, inspiration and divine influence? How would you argue?

What do you think is the most conducive environment for

maximizing creativity and human innovation? What about on a wider scale? Or historically? What about from a religious perspective? Or from a cultural point of view?

What are the most suitable circumstances for creativity?

What role does philosophy and art play in the process of creativity? What about spirituality? What about education, science or technology? What about the economy? Or politics?

What are the factors that inhibit creativity and implicitly innovation? What limits the human mind? For what reasons do you think people fail to understand things as they truly are, and to know as much as possible? What prevents human beings from doing all that they can in this life, here and now, or from trying to make the world a better place for future generations? What determines people to endure things the way they are? How would you compare the general situation with your specific context?

What role does curiosity play in creativity? What are the factors that stimulate or negatively impact it?

Who is the center of the universe? If man, man without God, or man thanks to God? If man is not the answer, who/what else?

What new boundaries should be crossed in order to improve the quality of life?

Do you think there is perfect divine order for long-lasting development? How would you argue your answer?

How would human thinking become more liberated and empowered to *discover the beauty, the wonder and the significance of every possible phenomenon, reason and science, in the search of new knowledge, meanings and values*?

What if human capacity would not be seen in opposition to the belief in the supernatural, but on the contrary, it would even be supported by it?

Practical Creativity

What kind of creative activities are you passionate about?

In what area could you be more creative?

How creative have you been this week? In what way would you improve?

For the following week, how much time would you invest in improving your creativity? What about the next season?

1.6. LIFESTYLE

What are the specific aspects of your lifestyle?

How organized and planned are you? How spontaneous and flexible? Do you prefer a routine?

What determines the rhythm of your life the most? What kind of hobbies do you have?

How would your life be if your vision were fulfilled?

What lessons have you learned from your leadership experience?

What lessons have you learned from your own leaders? What about by interacting or observing other leaders?

In your team, do you tend to direct or to delegate others?

How well does your leading style suit those you lead?

What leadership strengths do you have? What about your weaknesses?

As a visionary leader, how quickly do you go from directing to delegating?

How responsible do you feel for the tasks you delegate?

How do you express your responsibility for the tasks you delegate?

How do you offer your support and supervision?

What are the healthy boundaries you want to have between yourself and others?

As a visionary leader, how much do you tend to overload your team with new projects?

If your team would not be required to follow to you anymore, would they still want to?

How motivated is your team to complete the task they were initially given?

If you were offered another leadership job with more personal benefits, how willing would you be to give up your current project?

What offer would make you reconsider to continue in the current mission for which you still have dedication?

For what misconduct would you consider firing the best man on your team?

For what opportunities would you be ready to let go the best men on your team, solely for their own good?

What do you think would empower the newcomers on your team to accomplish extraordinary things?

Motivation

What are your inner ambitions, which you may only know yourself?

From the point of view of your best version, in what order would you list your ambitions?

Which of these would you like to share with someone close? What about publicly?

As a visionary, what is the area with which you identify the most? What about the first subdomain? Would you like to be even more specific in focus?

If you were to express the vision you would want to pursue all your life, and finally succeed in seeing it become a reality, what would it be?

If overnight you became the richest man in the world, in what would you invest your wealth mainly? For what purpose? What would be the next investment?

What role does money play in establishing your vision? How does the lack or abundance of money affect your vision?

If money was not a problem, would your vision be any different?

In the estimated impact of your vision, what role does the increase of your wealth play?

Reflection

On a scale of 0 to 10, to what extent does your current vision relate to your own human need to feel truly important?

What is the source of your value? How much does it depend on your performance or on the opinions of those around you?

Do you want to do great things to become more valuable, or precisely because you are already valuable you will do great things? Regardless of your own performance and other human validations?

Passion

What was your main passion in the past?

What are you passionate about today?

What are the first three verbs describing your passion?

Are they reflected in your work? What about in your plans?

How did your passion change or evolve in the past years?

How have things from your past contributed to your passion or to your current vision?

Reflection

How much of your free time do you spend doing what you are passionate about? How much would you like it to be? What would make that possible?

How much of your working time do you spend doing what you are passioned about? What about doing activities that are related to your passion? What about doing things (required) that have nothing to do with your passion?

How much time would you like to spend for each of the three categories?

What could you change about your program in order for you to spend more time doing what you are passioned about?

2. QUESTIONS FOR DIFFERENT TYPES OF PERSONALITY

What are your preferences?

Coaching Questions According to your personality type.

This section is essential to understand the following:

Why are some questions more relevant to some than others?

How does our personality type affect our preferences and concerns?

What contribution does our personality have to future success?

What are your strengths according to your personality type and how could you practice them more?

How could you be more strategic in choosing the people you want to accomplish your vision with?

How could you relate better and more efficiently to others?

2.1. MYERS BRIGGS

8/16 Types[2]

We are about to focus on eight of the 16 personality types, specifically those that are more Intuitive than Sensing.
The other eight types, which are more sensing than intuitive can be very useful in accomplishing a vision. We elaborate that in the second part of this book.

I/E: Introversion Or Extroversion - What Is Your Source Of Energy?

Being by yourself relaxes you more than being with others?

Do you tend to conserve your energy or consume it?

Would you rather have a few close friends or a wide circle of friends?

Are you a detached person, or more of an outgoing person?

Do you prefer solitude, or parties? What do you prefer between complexity and amplitude?

Do you assimilate better internally or through interaction? Would you rather focus or discuss?

N/S: Intuition Or Sensation-How Do You Perceive The Information?

Is it easier for you to see **the big picture**, or the broader, more general situation?

Are you more **theoretical** or more practical? **Innovative** or pragmatic? More of a dreamer or more factual? **Imaginative** or sentient?

Do you prefer the **future** or the present?

Would you rather seek **possibilities** or face the reality?

Are you the kind of person to look for **hidden meanings** or do you only believe what you see?

> *How could you cultivate more of your intuitive part in leadership?[3]*

How much does it help to keep in mind the big picture? What (type of) specific details do you tend to overlook? What helps you to keep in mind the whole picture?

How well do you manage to identify patterns? What about trends and future possibilities? How could you value this skill more?

How much do you live and lead into the future? How do you influence others personal growth and the systems around you?

How systematic and strategic is your thinking? What is the best environment for you to express this way?

How much do you manage to implement from the unlimited possibilities you see for the future?

How can you reduce the risk of dreaming without achieving?

How could you improve your leadership potential?

How can you compensate for your sensing side? With What?

T/F: Thinking Or Feeling – How Do You Make Decisions?

Do you prefer objective criteria, or it depends on their effect on people?

Do you tend to be more detached or more involved?

Do you prefer justice or harmony? Fairness or empathy? Law or mitigating circumstances?

Do you focus on principles / rules or values / qualities?

Does the argument matter more than convincing the others? Logic or instinct?

How can you cultivate your objective part more in leadership?[4]

How much do you manage to make unbiased decisions? How well do you use the cause-effect logic to reach a conclusion?

How analytical are you? How could you reach more clarity using objectivity, logic and analysis?(weigh carefully)

In the decision-making process, how do you avoid considering or communicating that those involved or affected are negligible, unimportant, or worthless?

Do you like solving problems? How much are you concerned with performance and improvements? While heading towards success, how do you avoid being too critical or insensitive?

How do you maintain relationships in the workplace? What is your way of prioritizing people?

P/J: Perception Or Organization – What Lifestyle Do You Prefer?

Do you prefer to keep your options open, or to have a stable routine? Do you resonate with undefined or clearly defined conclusions?

Do you tend to assimilate information without evaluating it or not? Do you tend to postpone deadlines or not?

Do you like to improvise along the way, or plan ahead?

Do you prefer flexibility or consistency? Adventure or clear expectations? Adaptation or control? Spontaneity or structuring and planning?

❖ ❖ ❖

NT Temperament: Intuition and thinking – rational, analyst[5]

Are you motivated towards efficiency? Are you inventive, strategic and future-oriented? Do you think systematically and conceptually? Are you an independent thinker who tends to establish his capacity? Do you like to solve problems in an analytic way, taking into account the basic principles? Do you often learn from debates?

How important is it for you to be competent? How likely are

you to set your own standards of competence and excellence?

How much do you like to theorize and intellectualize?

How much would you like to understand how things work?

How much are you concerned with a better way of doing things?

How much do you like adventure and risk?

How natural is it to provoke decision makers?

How natural is it to test the system and the state of affairs?

How natural is it to be critical of yourself, but also of others?

How much do others perceive you as distant or "intellectual"?

How easy is it for you to see the big picture?

How good do you see yourself at conceptualizing? What about systematic planning?

How solid do you consider yourself to be in your internal logic? What about in matters of principles of systems and organizations?

How able are you to express yourself clearly and accurately?

How much does it matter to you to have interesting discussions?

How does debating help you in your learning process?

Did it happen to you to get lost in strategies, at the risk of neglecting an everyday matters?

Entp Leader [6]: Visionary, Inventor, Debater – Yet Another Challenge!

Are you ingenious, inventive and fast? Are you attracted to new possibilities and ideas? Are you testing boundar-

ies? Entrepreneurial, friendly, competitive and challenging? Eager for growth but tired of details and routines?

How do you feed your inventiveness? How much do you fructify it?

How do you handle your new ideas? What about new challenges?

How could you practice your ideas more?

In what context could you generate as many creative alternatives as possible? In favor of what kind of system would you like to contribute? What is the criterion for filtering them?

How do you cope with the challenge of pursuing a super idea in a focused manner in order to translate it into reality? What about choosing the optimal way of implementation?

How can you avoid delays or even unfulfilled dreams?

What attracts you to take up on adventurous roles?

How do you manage risks when it comes to resources?

What was the most adventurous decision you ever made?

What adventurous business would you want to get involved in? How would you like to initiate something like that?

In the next project, for what reason do you think you can win on a large scale? Why do you think you could never lose?

How often do find yourself testing the boundaries of the surrounding systems? What about those of the most traditional people?

How much time do you spend discussing and coming up with new ideas?

How often do you test the reaction of others by what you say or do?

What kind of people do you prefer to interact with?

In which group where you can make the best exchange of ideas, arguments, challenges and projects?

To develop yourself, how could you be more of a player and less of a spectator? How exciting would that be?

What should happen in order for your involvement to be followed by useful, noticed and shared results?

What kind of people would benefit most from interacting with you?

What kind of people do you think can help you improve?

How likely is this competitiveness of yours to be perceived by some as bullying or becoming tiresome to others? Especially for whom?

In your working environment, how do you get more accuracy, planning, order and stability? Who do you count on?

How likely are you to accept being held accountable? What if you started your own accountability relationship? How would that help you?

How can you allot more time for creativity? What about space?

In what would you like to invest more time? How do you usually waste your time?

What stimulates your creativity? What inhibits it?

How do you protect your imagination and your creativity from tedious details? What about boring routines?

What could you do at your workplace that would feel like a challenge?

How do you deal with standard operational procedures?

To what extent do you deal with the following areas: computer science, financial investment consulting, teaching in an education system, etc.? What other theoretical concerns do you have?

When does the time for introspection come? What about to appreciate what your senses tell you, or for more emotional moments in life?

Entj Leader [7]: Manager, Innate Leader – Leading For The Better!

Are you consistent, argumentative and vigorous? Thinker but interactive? Do you learn by debating? Are you sincere, decisive, well-informed, positive but self-critical and impatient? Happy to feel challenged, excellent communicator, open and direct?

When do you really feel the need to be in control?

What kind of systems have you created so far? What about products?

If your world were a chess board, how would you feel to be the one moving the pieces?

How much do you understand the system of management around you? How accessible are they to you?

How much do you use your argumentation to grow?

What does a constructive confrontation look like to you? What about from the perspective of the less competitive?

How important is it for you to be challenged? What about the outcome of the challenge?

What do you perceive those who challenge you intellectually, or in any other way? What about those who refuse your challenges?

How do you think those who feel intimidated by you perceive you?

What makes you lose your patience?

How do you react when those around you complain about insignificant things?

What are the things you usually consider more important, significant and better? How do you feel when they concern you?

How true is it that you don't like details? Or that you don't excel in interpersonal matters?

How do you respond to criticism?

How do you value your communication skills?

How could you have even more open, more honest, and more stimulating relationships?

How willing are you to give time for your relationships to grow stronger?

How often do you plan spare time for you to relax?

What do you think is your best quality that helps you be a better leader?

In what situations do you feel like an innate leader?

Where do you practice the most leadership skills?

How much do you value your systematic planning skills?

What is the most distant date planned on the agenda? How about an even bolder one?

What are the most important things you are planning strategically?

By the way, when are you going to give yourself more time for reflection and contemplation? What about to be less busy and less *plugged in*?

What do you do in situations where you could hurt people in

the pursuit of goals? How do you help others not to take things too personally?

What would you do if your leadership ambitions were at the expense of your team? What would you firstly work on? What about on your communication skills?

Intp Leader [8]: Logical, Architect – There Are More Solutions To Any Problem

> *Do you like to solve problems? Are you reflective, logical, analytical, conceptual, reserved, but very flexible? Do you see many perspectives? Do you integrate different points of view? Do you enjoy a theoretical debate?*

How often do you happen to overthink an idea?

When someone shares an idea with you, do you feel like you have just been invited to explore, debate and rethink it?

How easy is it for you to solve the next "new problem"? What about doing more things all at once?

Beyond studying a particular subject, how much do you enjoy the learning and development process?

How much do you appreciate independent thinking and intellectual development? How do you encourage it?

How often do you prefer to offer suggestions than to impose your ideas?

How often do you happen to keep trying to form a whole (which seems to be expanding – article, plan, schema or theory) from a growing multitude of data?

How much do you want to adapt your life to a theoretical

model?

How much do you like the process of improving your own work? What about compared to finishing the work itself?

Are you accustomed to making last-minute adjustments? In such situations, who might not share the same enthusiasm?

After you have almost accomplished perfection, how do you feel to be the first to criticize your own work for better results?

How much do you value your intelligence and competence while facing imperfections? What about self-control on your path to excellence?

What do you do when your own ambitious goals tend to overload you mentally?

How often do you take mental challenges as part of focusing on a project?

What do you do when you deal with activities that do not involve too much brainpower, skill and refinement?

What helps you focus when you started conceptualizing? In what situations do you easily sink yourself in processing and reflecting? In such moments, what do you tend to neglect?

What opportunities for exploration, understanding and growth are most accessible to you? What about ideally?

In designing a plan or a project, which aspects are vital?

How much would intermediate deadlines help you transition and progress?

When are you going to spend more time for externalization? What about for more subjectivity and feelings?

When would you like to make a difference on a larger scale with your thinking and ideas? Through what?

Through what questions would you appeal people to explore more? Who would you consider?

Intj Leader [9]: Brilliant, Strategist, Independent – Improving Everything

> *Are you serious and intense? Do you organize and run systems? Determined to stubbornness? Extremely independent, self-motivated and innovative? Do you feel tense until you make it happen? Do you learn by debating?*

How much are you stubborn when it comes to your own way of thinking and acting?

What is your latest ambition or vision that you ponder even in the form of relaxation?

How much do you enjoy making improvements?

What are the areas where you are constantly improving things?

What area concerns you even though you know you cannot control it?

In what field do you think you could be the brains behind the development?

As a leader of which system do you think you could make the biggest difference? Where exactly?

How likely is it for you to be the founder of a system?

Although you are able to also see the trees, not just the forest, which of the two categories takes up the most time? On what would you like to spend more time?

What is the most significant thing you have done so far?

How does a well job look like for you? What about a well-articulated message?

What is the biggest opportunity you have gotten so far?

In what situations do you feel the most confident?

Do you happen to be misunderstood while you're making improvements? Or while discussing objectively a hot topic?

How independent do you tend to be, compared to the people around you? What are the strengths of an independent person such as you are? What about the risks?

Who could complete you best and lead you to success?

Due to what qualities would people find you inspiring? In what field? For whom? In what way?

Who would you be able to motivate to be more independent and responsible?

What is the project you have been working on lately? How can you keep yourself away from stagnation?

How do you prevent the intellectual enthusiasm with which you make ambitious plans from being frustrated by the lack of implementation?

What stimulates you intellectually the most? What about relationally? What consumes you the most?

In which place do you think your plan will come to life?

How do you relate to leaders when you are being led? How could you get more freedom and trust? What about more mental challenges and inventiveness space? Or less personal services?

When will you find more time for your own sensing fulfillment? What about for the more subjective-emotional side? Or for more spontaneity?

How much do you get inspired by socializing?

NF Temperament: Intuition and

feeling – idealistic, Diplomatic

Are you very concerned with the identity and the meaning of life? Do you tend to always see potential in others? Are you people-oriented, friendly and empathetic? Is harmony essential to you? Are you sensitive, articulated and enthusiastic? Do you like to support causes and help people? Are you good at encouraging others?

What is the basis of your identity?

How do you get even more inspiration?

What kind of causes have you supported so far?

What kind of causes are you passionate about? In whose favor? Against what?

Who would you like to promote? What kind of people would you like to make feel important and valuable? What about wise and happy?

What is one movement you want to be a part of?

What movement could you initiate? How much do you want it?

What gives you inner peace?

How do you manage to have more peacefulness around you?

How much do you use your ability to get the best out of the people you work with?

How much do you have the opportunity to be articulate and convincing? In what context?

How much do you have the desire to help others? Especially who?

Who can you help by encouraging them more? For whom is enough even a smile from you?

What do you do when the others don't have the same opinions as you?

Where would it be necessary for you to act more firmly or establish clear boundaries?

When would it be worth not to avoid a conflict? How do you avoid taking criticism too personally?

Enfp Leader: [10]Activist, Campaigner – Cultivating And Promoting

Are you friendly and caring? Do you see potential in others? Do you consider yourself enthusiastic and dynamic? Are you a creative, free and have a social spirit? Do you always find a reason to smile? Are you good at starting things? Do you have a rich imagination?

How do you value your tremendous ability to be concerned, even simultaneously, with a variety of people, events or challenges?

What kind of interpersonal dynamics make you feel most at ease?

How much do you like to assert others and be asserted? How do you avoid becoming dependent on the approval or the validation of others?

What exactly can you figure out from people's behavior?

What excites you the most? How could you experience this more? In what context?

What causes are you passionate about? What kind of causes do you already have plans for? How likely is it for you to start a campaign soon? What about to finish it? During a campaign, what are the factors that might cause you frustration? How could you organize yourself better?

What would be the most extensive campaign you would like to start?

What kind of people are you most likely to understand and accept them as they are? How are you perceived by these people? Are there any negative effects due to your identification with them?

Do you usually think you need to personally do something to have better relationships?

What should happen in order for you to help improve the society? How can you use your energy even better to help others achieve their goals? What would you do if your enthusiasm led you towards too many directions all at once?

How do you relax without too much effort? What creative adventure would relax you?

What kind of actions do you learn the most from? How do you best integrate your knowledge into the overall picture?

How could you combine work and your personal life as satisfactorily as possible? What about more efficiently?

In what situations do you have the chance to improvise the most?

In what situations do you tend to be too critical of yourself? What would make you truly pleased? How could you be more pleased with yourself? How could you be yourself more? How could you show that more? What actions can best express who you really are? How does your perfect environment look like?

In the long run how can you positively affect as many people as possible? How could you be more focused? What about persevere? Or to use objectivity more?

Enfj Leader: [11]Protagonist, Teacher, Motivator – Special Communicator

> *Do you like to inspire and motivate others? Are you a charismatic and intuitive leader, able to fascinate your audience? Are you full of life and create a good mood around you? Are you responsible and relational?*

What do you think is your best quality in a leadership position? Why do you think people would naturally follow you? What makes you a genuine leader?

How much do you value your communication skills, such as eloquence, motivation, persuasion? What about your skills to understand people and their motivations?

Towards what kind of people are you oriented in the first place? Or towards what kind of areas? What helps you grow in communication skills and not be shallow?

What helps you connect with the people you are addressing? How do you manage to meet their needs?

What do you think people need to act at their full potential? What role does the quality of relationships play?

How much do you like to lead a group or more? What do you think would qualify you to help others manage their relationships within organizations or institutions?

What pushes you to guide others in a certain direction? Generally, what does all the guiding come to? Towards what do you want to guide others the most?

What do you do when your ideas are met with resistance or rejection? How do you manage your feelings in situations of disagreement? How could you not take the rejection or the conflict too personally? How could you better manage any affronts? How do you avoid holding a grudge or resentment?

While you are a fascinating speaker, how good of a listener are you? How could you be better at both?

What are the values you think you can best convey to others? What do you think is the main cause of all the evil in the world? How do you motivate people to overcome it?

While you are positive and friendly, how do you handle a confrontation that is necessary?

How do you mix work with relaxation? What brings you joy outside of your work environment?

How do you show to those you work with that are important and valuable?

Who are your heroes and role models? How do they inspire you?

What makes you really feel involved in a group? How often do you have such opportunities?

What does it mean for you to cultivate your potential?

What type of activities do you find boring or tedious? How do you avoid exhaustion? What kind of people do usually complement you?

How can you spare a little more time for you to reflect? What about for more practical things?

Infp Leader: [12]Mediator, Healer – Noble Idealist At The Service Of Society

> Do you like to be benevolent and sympathetic to people? Are you always ready to help a good cause? Are you dedicated to justice but kind hearted? Do you have an inner

strength, but you are willing to be flexible too? Do you have a poetic and artistic sense with a strong desire for significance?

What is the noblest cause you have been involved in so far? Have you ever initiated one?

What rules do you live by? What do they come down to? How do you respect them?

How do you explain your tendency to be benevolent and sympathetic to people? Under what conditions do you manage to maximize this quality? Under what conditions do you have difficulties to express it?

How important is harmony to you, compared to stirring disagreements all around?

For what reason would you be willing to start a disagreement, no matter the consequences? What threatens your value system?

How much are you concerned that the people around you are treated with justice and fairness? Would you fight against an injustice in society? What about for a better environment?

Towards what would you like to channel all your efforts? How likely is it to achieve it soon? What would this ideal look like on a larger scale? Why would you be passionate about this?

What is the example that inspires you in pursuing such a noble ideal?

What really defines you? In what situations do you really feel like you are evolving? What kind of activities give you confidence? What does your daily effort contribute to? How could you further develop these quests?

What are your favorite topics for discussion?

How do you handle disagreements?

In what way would you like to grow more? How would that contribute more to your desired ideal?

How well do you manage your feelings? What about not internalizing them too much? How do you keep your mental health? How do you relax?

When do you feel like you have pleased others enough?

What do you do when your sacrifices are not appreciated enough?

Do you want to pursue a personal life and a career with integrity, understanding and concern for other people?

What are the aspects in which you tend to be critical of yourself? What about the others? What does excellence mean to you? In what field do you want to pursue it? What do you think really fulfils you?

In what way do you want to be at the service of people? In what area do you think you might be the most accomplished and productive?

Infj Leader: Advocate, [13] Lawyer, Counselor - Inspirational And Care For Others

Are you a quiet, dedicated, conscientious and persevering person? Do you live with intensity and desire to contribute to the good of others? Are you aiming to have ideals, values and a clear vision? Are you good at group networking? Do you have a rich inner life? Are you tidy and creative?

In what situations are you the most gentle, compassionate and accepting? In what situations are you stubborn or even rigid?

What is your biggest humanitarian concern? For what kind of goals are you willing to fight with the greatest determination and perseverance?

What dream do you have that has the potential of inspiring others? What is specific about your brilliance?

What are your deepest or most intense concerns? What kind of interaction is your inner strength expressed in? What helps you to externalize it? Who believes the most in your potential?

What are your limits for hope, aspirations and care for others? When do you reach these limits?

How much do you value your skills regarding group dynamics? What kind of issues do you manage to read very quickly in a group interaction? What are the things where you have a higher level of awareness than others? What could this help you with? What about the people in question?

How could you develop your communication skills more? First in relation to whom?

How natural is it to make yourself vulnerable when it comes to your own needs?

How could you make your ideas more valuable?

What would you like to do for more harmony around you?

In what area are you the most stimulating, resourceful and helpful to others? How do you contribute to growth and development?

What stimulates you intellectually the most?

For a leadership position, how do you manage to show maximum concern for both people and their products or services? How could you better express your appreciation for team members? How could you motivate them better? How can you highlight their strengths to help them achieve their goals?

How do you handle possible work conflicts and tension in interpersonal relationships?

How do you get more time for your own dreams and moments of inspiration and creativity? How could you delegate more of your tasks?

What is the most ambitious project or role in which you want to excel at?

SP Temperament: Sensation and Perception – Explorer, artisan[14]

Are you very motivated to experience life just like that? Are you spontaneous, pragmatic? Do you like being flexible and living in the present? Do you learn while experimenting? Do you prefer the action? Good implementer, though not the most structured? Tolerant and quite relaxed, but skillful and practical?

ESTP, ESFP, ISTP, ISFP

How much does it matter to you to be original and to keep up with the contemporary generation?

How much do you enjoy the present?

What does a fun day mean to you?

How can you inspire others to enjoy life? What would you like to give to the people around you? In what specific way? What would be the next key move?

How willing are you to take risks?

What makes you embrace emergencies that others flee from?

How much do you value your technical skills?

What do you know how to fix best? Where could you do that

more? What are other areas related to that?

Where do you value your negotiating ability? In what situations?

What practical problems do you like to solve the most? What could you possibly excel in?

What are the resources you can acquire faster than many others?

For what kind of crises could you immediately generate concrete solutions?

What best meets your need to act purposefully?

How intense do you like to live your life? How does that fit with the close ones? How many love your style and how many do not?

As you excel in immediate matters how could you get more predictability and structure?

How do you expand your development in more practical areas? What about in the most theoretical?

What intellectual matters interest you? How could they bring you more satisfaction?

How could you manage your finances better?

SJ Temperament: Sensation and organization[15] – Protector, reliable man

You bring stability around? Does the respect for duties, tradition and responsibilities characterizes you? Are you practical, diligent, responsible, trustworthy, loyal? Do you like to help your team? Are you good at implementation and in administration? Do you know how to respect au-

thority?

ESTJ, ESFJ, ISTJ, ISFJ

What was the most important project you organized?

What do you like to organize more: people, objects, programs, organizations, etc.?

Where do you think organized people are the most needed?

In what places should there be more people like you?

Who is in great need of your ability to implement appropriate procedures?

Where would your organizational skills stand out the most? What about your skills of taking the initiative and bringing clarity?

How much does it matter to you to know who is responsible?

How does a productive day look like for you?

How do you ensure that while you are very involved in the present, you do not neglect other future responsibilities?

What are the roles you prefer the most? What about the ones you dislike?

What brings you the most stability?

How do you keep the stability around you? Where is it most needed? Where could you show a little more flexibility?

What helps you persevere in fulfilling your promises?

How could you be more involved in resource management?

How do you make sure you continue to learn new things?

What project, business or organization would you start that would become a success for sure?

2.2. DISC

Four Dimensions[16]

Disc Model[17]

Dominant – How do you manage problems and control situations?

Influent – How do you manage relationships with people? How do you communicate? How do you relate to others?

Stability – how patient, persevering and caring are you?

Conformity – How do you address and organize your work, procedures and responsibilities?

Which of the 15 DISK profiles characterizes you best[18]?

The ambitious, the coach, the counselor, the creative, the enthusiastic, the evaluator, the individualist, the inspirational, the investigator, the objective, the perfectionist, the leader, the practician, the results-oriented, or the specialist?

[19] Which of the 8 DISK leading styles characterizes you best?

Pioneer (Di, Id), Energetic (I), Assertive (Is, Si), inclusive(S), Modest (Sc, Cs), Deliberate (C), Determined (Cd, Dc), or Imposing (D)?

2.3. ENNEAGRAM

Nine Types[20]

According To The Quick Test (Quest)

Which description characterizes you best[21]?

From group I: A, B, or C?
From group II: X, Y, or Z?

According to the corresponding two letters, what's your personality type?

In Leadership,[22]

 i. What are your strengths?
 ii. What are your challenges?
 iii. How could you grow better?

Ax – 7: The Enthusiastic, The Generalist

 i. How could you maximize your leadership through "innovation, high energy, generating ideas, enthusiasm, curiosity and engagement"?
 ii. How do you cope with the challenge of "being impulsive and unfocused, avoiding difficult problems, rationalizing and lack of well-chosen follow-up steps"?

  iii. How could you "learn to forgive and forget, listen more, sit still and focus on execution as much as generating ideas?"

Ay – 8: The Ruler

  i. How could you maximize your leadership through "strategic vision, understanding of networks of influence, honesty, audacity and action"?
  ii. How do you cope with the challenge of "being controlling and demanding, agitated by the slow pace or lack of large-scale and over-extended actions"?
  iii. How could you "learn to forgive and forget, taking into account that there are several valid perspectives and to appreciate conversations"?

Az – 3: The One Who Succeeds, The Competitive

  i. How could you maximize your leadership through "clear goals, focus, entrepreneurship, the energy and the attitude" we can do it "?
  ii. How do you cope with the challenge of "being overly competitive, abrupt when stressed, impatient with long conversations and overworked"?
  iii. How could you not exaggerate in "identifying yourself too much with your work, as the main meaning of who you are and the value you bring to the table"?

Bx – 9: Pacifier, Mediator

  i. How could you maximize your leadership through "diplomacy, consensus, inclusion, patience, respect for others and consistency"?
  ii. How do you cope with the challenge of "being

insecure, avoiding conflict, too yielding and undecided or with low energy"?
iii. How could you develop more by "believing in yourself, being more confident in what you have to offer as a leader and sharing your point of view with the others"?

By – 4: Individualist, Artist

i. How could you maximize your leadership through "vision based on values, creativity, inspiration, compassion, and interpersonal connection"?
ii. How do you cope with the challenge of "being too intense or too sentimental, too sensitive and quiet"?
iii. How could you grow more "focusing less on yourself, on your feelings and others and more on the task at hand"?

Bz – 5: Thinker, Observer

i. How could you maximize your leadership through "research and planning, perspectives and logical analysis, objectivity and expertise"?
ii. How do you cope with the challenge of "being detached, distant, too independent, to be uncomfortable in getting involved with others, and being overly cerebral"?
iii. How could you grow more by "expressing your emotional state more and trusting your own instincts"?

Cx – 2:The Helper, The Altruist

i. How could you maximize your "leadership

through motivation, the development of excellent relationships, support and inventiveness for resources"?
ii. How do you cope with the challenge of "being overly focused on relationships, having difficulty saying *no* or setting boundaries, and being too involved"?
iii. How could you grow more by "focusing on tasks as well as on the relational aspects of leadership, by taking more time to rest, eat and relax"?

Cy – 6: Devoted, Loyal

i. How could you maximize your leadership through "collaboration, creative problem solving, risk assessment, loyalty and perseverance"?
ii. How do you cope with the challenge of "being too cautious in taking risks, and being too conformist or too intransigent, projecting feelings and thoughts on others"?
iii. How could you grow more by "asking less often: "*what if*" and much more "*why not*" as you approach challenges as a leader?"

Cz – 1: The Reformate, The Perfectionist

i. How could you maximize your leadership by "leading by example, organization, consistency, responsibility, pragmatism and attention to detail"?
ii. How do you cope with the challenge of being "reactive and critical, excessively involved in operational details, opinionated and inflexible"?
iii. How could you grow more by "learning to delegate, even the work that pleases you, without con-

stantly checking on others"?

3. VISIONARY LEADER

How do you tend to lead?

3.1. AWARENESS AND POSITIONING

If all the leaders were like you, how would that reflect in the contemporary society? What kind of culture would essentially be promoted?

Firmness Or Flexibility

After the decisions have already been made, to what extent do you keep them intact, and how much do you tend to adjust them?

In general, what is your tendency, in terms of maintaining decisions or readjusting them?

In what areas do you prefer intransigence and where you prefer flexibility?

How intransigent would you be if your leadership team asked you to readjust your initial vision?

How flexible would you be about mission implementation strategies?

If you had something to gain from the adjustment of the vision, what would you change? In what way?

How do you limit your vision or your mission?

Which limits are non-negotiable? Which can be extended? Which can be restricted?

What are the limits to success you have not thought you could overcome (though you will)?

Why would you need to overcome them?

In what way does that depend on you?

What are the things you could do to succeed? Firstly...?

What limiting beliefs do you have?

How willing are you to defend your beliefs at any price?

What are the criteria after which you adjust your beliefs?

How do you know when a belief limits your long-term growth?

To what perspective do you tend to be skeptical?

What are your beliefs that make you very confident that you will win in the long run, even at the risk of short term losses?

3.2. VISIONARY MENTALITY

This section is for: reflection, self-knowledge, rational exploration, discoveries, etc. The implementation part will be reflected more specifically in the next chapter, about exploring the society, in order to be more prepared to shape the vision elaborated in Chapter Five.

> *Did it ever happen to you that after presenting a brilliant idea to a group, it would be immediately lynched by the majority? Have you reconciled with the thought that truly innovative ideas do not create instant consensus? Do you happen to have thoughts beyond conventional wisdom?*

What are the characteristics of innovative thinking? How could you think in a more visionary manner? How could you rationalize innovation better? How could you be more creative?

Wealthy Mentality[23][24]

How conscious are you of your inner wealth?

Does wealth create a rich mindset, or does a rich mindset create wealth?

If your possessions would be taken away from you, how rich would you still be?

What is your source of inner well-being?

What nourishes your visionary spirit? What energizes you mentally? What gives you hope?

Beyond social status, achievements and possessions, how noble or royal do you see yourself as a human being?

Without being arrogant, how could you not underestimate your importance and your inner value?

How could you reflect your inner riches externally?

How could you externalize your importance and value without being selfish?

How could you enhance your ability to create and multiply wealth?

What mental boundaries do people put in the way of their potential? What if people's mentality keeps them in poverty?

What boundaries have you crossed so far? What limits are you going to exceed?

How can you think in a prosperous manner in order to manage your relationships, roles, responsibilities and resources better?

Without showing off, how much are you willing to spend when it comes to taking care of your own basic needs?

How much does quality and aesthetics matter to you?

Without being a snob or superficial, how do you avoid minimalist aspirations?

In what aspects is it okay for you to be catalogued as an elitist?

If modesty means having the right opinions about yourself, what qualities of yours would it be okay to boast?

What skills would make you feel confident in facing a competition with those in a league considered superior?

With what inborn and refined talent do you know you could contribute in an elite group?

How do you report to failure and suffering? How could you do it better?

How do you manage the risks? What about criticism and conflict?

How well do you make the most of your time? With how much wisdom?

How much do you train mentally?

What mental abilities would you like to cultivate?

How do you develop your emotional intelligence?

What aspects of poor mentality, or mediocrity do you still tend to have? How could you act in the opposite spirit?

How much do you think God is in your favor, wanting you to thrive? How much do you consider yourself connected to the divinity to really think prosperously? How empowered do you consider yourself?

Generally speaking, what are the valid principles for you to thrive? How do you know?

> *Who are the people who inspire you to cultivate a rich mentality? How does your entourage look like? For whom are you a source of inspiration?*

What do you think is the main cause of poverty? What would the first three be?

Contesting The Status Quo[25]

How could you extend the conventional boundaries?

How often do you dare to question the assumptions and beliefs of others? Usually, of what kind? What unconventional potential do you tend to explore? With how much wisdom?

How do you know when a generally accepted issue is erroneous? How much are you willing to go against the tide? What new skeptical questions are you concerned about? What popular belief can you challenge? What about a widespread disbelief? Or harmful ignorance?

"What if God actually wants us to use our mastermind and creative capabilities that He has given us, to their full potential"? (Francesco Petrarca)

What if... [you were to think against the tide in the area that concerns you most]?

How much do you assess the assumptions of others?

How much do you test conventional thinking in your area of responsibility? What about the next level, or the context you are part of? How could you manifest a more constructive criticism? What principles help you?

Harnessing Trends[26]

How do you use current trends for the evolution you grasp?

How much do you notice the trends around you? What about those in more cutting-edge areas? How much do you expose yourself to new and inspiring perspectives?

How much connected are you to the latest news in the industry?

How often do you notice changes in the society or in your field of interest?

How much do you want to be the key factor in positive trend changes?

What elements of novelty would you like to bring?

What is the ideal which your organization or society could embrace?

Channeling Resources[27]

How could you put all your resources together?

How much do you appreciate what you have, while pursuing new achievements?

How often do you care to value relationships, skills and assets you already have, to develop new ones? What about channeling them to achieve something different?

How much are you aware of the unlimited ability to develop, expand, combine and channelize resources?

How can you value more what you have, what you know and what you can do? What about in your relationships with the others? How much does it hurt you that people suffer because they neglect some of their own capacities and resources?

Understanding The Needs[28]

How much are you concerned to find relevant solutions to the needs ignored by most? What about the possibility to approach the current needs more skillfully? What kind of needs are you worried about in the first place?

How much do you cultivate your curiosity and concern for the world around you? What about the belief that you can make the world a better place? How responsible do you feel to improve the quality of life of the people around you?

How often do you think about problems where no one seems to be looking for real or more effective solutions? What about the ones that the majority is not even aware of? How could you connect unfulfilled needs with innovation and development opportunities?

How much do you carefully observe the surrounding reality? How intentionally? How could you become a better observer? How often are you concerned with identifying and solving problems that seem unsolvable? What about to combine what is necessary with what is possible? What would help you figure out these two issues better?

How much do you want to find a better approach? Generally speaking, how much do you manage to meet the people's needs? How could you do a better job?

How much empathy do you have towards those in need? How often do you do something about it? Do you know not to waste your energy in times of need? Nevertheless, how much do you prove you actually care?

What questions do you have about your current situation?

How focused are you on understanding the needs of your organization? What about the emerging ones?

3.3. LEADERSHIP STYLES

Situational Leadership[29]

How much do you (aim to) intervene to perform the necessary tasks?

How often do you (tend to) tell people what they should do, how, when and where?

How is your relational behavior?

How relational do you consider yourself? What do others say about you, in this regard?

How important is it for you to be the friend of those you lead? In choosing the team members, who would appreciate it the most to be chosen as a part of the team?

How natural does it feel to you to establish a friendly relationship with people?

How much and how well do you communicate?

How much: Do you listen, encourage, clarify and provide support?

How available are your team members?

How reliable are your team members to accomplish a particular task? Do they have the knowledge, the experience and the skills to succeed in doing a task or an activity?

How eager are your team members to perform given tasks? How much confidence, dedication and motivation do they have to finish a task or an activity?

How do you adapt to your team members according to their availability?

What do you tackle team members who lack skills and availability? In this situation, what are the advantages of a more authoritative style? What would help them develop?

How do you lead those who have less skills and availability? What kind of *guidance* is it necessary? How could you provide explanations and opportunities for clarification?

What do you do with those who have the skills but they are not eager to fulfill their duties? How could you encourage them or have a conversation asking them to put in more effort?

How do you lead those who are eager lack in skills to perform their duties? How could you stimulate their potential?

How do you relate to those who are both capable and eager? How could you delegate and empower them more?

Leadership: Transactional Vs Transformational[30]

Are you primarily action oriented, or do you tend to use a higher degree of vision?

Are you more concerned with tasks and relationships, or with your vision and then the action?

Transactional Leadership

Do you tend to interfere only when the team members do not perform to your expectations?

Do you tend to give only negative feedback?

To motivate your team, do you only use rewards conditioned by performances?

Transformational Leadership

Are you setting clear goals? Do you encourage your team members to use their own capabilities and resources?

Do you provide intellectual stimulation for personal innovation?

Are you a source of inspiration? Are you known for your principles? Do you encourage people to seek new possibilities?

Do you give importance to all team members in a personalized way?

Does the pursuing of your vision and your mission make you charismatic? Are you a role model for your team? Are you respected and trusted?

Altruistic Leadership

How preoccupied are you to help the people you interact with? What about the people from whom you cannot get something in return?

How much do you intend (or how much do you want) to inspire the people around to dare more, to reach their full potential and purpose?

How willing are you to offer concrete (launching) opportunities to those you inspire?

How willing are you to assist the people you promote?

Who is the one person you would like to invest the most? Who would be the next one?

How much are you willing to share your leadership tips and tricks?

Use Of Power

How could you create more leaders than followers, or simple contributors?

How much do you believe in team leadership?

What are the advantages of a long-term leadership?

How could you empower people even more?

How could you involve more people in leadership?

Who would be the right person you would give more responsibilities to?

What is the connection between power and authority?

Authority

What is the source of your authority?

What is the difference between positional and personal authority?

Between the authority based on a position (or function or title) and the personal one, which one do you tend to use more?

If tomorrow you lose any positional authority, how would it affect you?

How many of your team would follow you only for your personal authority?

To what extent do you agree that the genuine authority comes more from what you are than what you know or what you do? Which of the three was the most encouraged in the education system you grew up in?

How do you want to increase your personal authority?

Do you agree that for you to have authority you must be under an authority?

What is the connection between authority and respect? What about between authority and influence?

How do you want to increase your authority? Trying to keep it to yourself, or sharing it with the team?

In leadership, do you see yourself as a leader OF a group of people, or rather FOR those people? What is the difference?

4. EXPLORING THE SOCIETY

where do you find yourself?

Each visionary leader wants to make a major difference in society. Some focus on the whole society, others on a specific aspect, but with applicability in several areas of the society.

First, we will explore the main areas of the society at the macro level.

Then we will look at the society, at the micro level, using the five specific strengths of the visionary mentality, from the previous chapter.

4.1. 10 AREAS OF SOCIETY

What is your area of influence?

Business

What measures would you take as a new Minister of Economy or as the Minister of Business Environment? For what would you like to be known? What strategic priorities would you have?

What measures would you take as mayor?

What are your criteria for prioritizing? What should you keep in mind?

What would your priorities be?

How would you stimulate your local business environment?

Currently, in what way do local businesses contribute to the community development? How satisfying?

How could local businesses contribute more to the community development? What about in another context, in another less developed location?

Do businesses have the potential to transform the quality of life, of families, communities, and even nations?

How could these eliminate poverty? What about increasing individual prosperity?

How could living standards be increased?

What could sustain the long-term economic growth? What values and principles? What are the pillars of a strategic development?

What are the main indicators of economic development?

What is the political context? What about the training of the workforce?

How does the international context affect the local one?

What are the long-term development prospects? What aspects are overestimated? What about underestimated?

How could the development of private businesses be encouraged? What about local partnerships?

What are the downsides of the current approach? What potential is wasted by the current approach?

How do social factors affect the business environment? What about the other way around?

What are the key areas for the future?

How could the quality of life of a group of people improve?

How could people have more of a good mood, not just more material prosperity?

What is missing from the local business environment? What about in the broader context?

How much does the trust deficit in a specific domain cost? How could honesty and transparency increase?

What are the most critical factors affecting the business environment?

What challenges regarding the system does an experienced

business person have? What about one at the beginning of the career?

What needs do business people have?

What are the current trends in the business sphere?

What are the opportunities?

What innovation would help many businesses simultaneously?

What mistakes do many business people make?

How could new business opportunities be found?

How could the demand be better met with the offer?

How could more jobs be created?

How could the human potential be better capitalized?

What would an economic approach look like in which people's vocation and personality are more important than immediate profit?

How could businesses be done more intentionally? And more relationally?

How could businesses be done with more excellency in ethics and practice?

How could businesses be more sustainable? What are the main reasons for failure?

How could business be less dependent on a single man?

How could human exploitation and dehumanization be avoided?

How could more value be added to work?

How could the prices be more competitive? How could the costs be reduced?

What kind of work could be automated?

How could better working conditions be created?

How could the resources be better used? Where is time, energy and other resources being wasted?

What areas are left behind? What systems and structures are outdated?

In what areas is there a crisis of trained personnel?

How could there be better investments in infrastructure and in preparing leaders?

How to better facilitate collaboration and cooperation between several entities (private and governmental; personal and institutional)?

How can internships at the workplace be facilitated?

How could an extra quality and trust be brought?

What business is your cup of tea?

What job would you prefer? What is the role you are targeting?

Technology: The Industries of the future

Which industries do you think have the greatest potential for growth and profitability? What are the trends? What are the opportunities and the challenges to reach the next level of engagement?

What is the potential for renewable energy?

What is the potential for virtual reality?

What is the potential for biotechnology? What about other technologies?

What is the potential for artificial intelligence?

What is the potential for leisure?

What are other industries of the future?

Science

How much is invested in education and research, for economic development? How well is it done?

What are the issues left behind in relation to current perspectives?

What should be the strategic priorities?

How could education and research be facilitated in specific economic branches?

What are the current trends in the area that you are interested in?

What future problems or opportunities could be encountered by investing in education and research?

What do you think you should really do? What are you going to do?

Education

What measures would you take as a new Minister of Education?

What measures would you take as a school headmaster?

What is your criteria for setting priorities? What should you keep in mind?

What would your priorities be?

Among the priorities of a country, what role does education play? How should this be reflected in the annual budget?

What do you think is the role of education in society?

What is the role of the family and what is the school's role? How should the two cooperate?

What are the key elements in the education system?

What are the alternatives to the classic system?

What is lacking from the contemporary approach?

What are the critical aspects of the learning approach?

What should be changed in order for the student to go to school with pleasure?

How much are students praised by teachers?

How close is the relationship between the teacher and the student?

How could the teacher win the student's trust?

How could the student respect the teacher more?

How could the school offer be more diversified to better meet the specifics of the students?

How could certain schools specialize in certain areas?

How could schools collaborate with each other in favor of the student and the locale community?

What would a complementary offer in education look like with various options for the student?

How much is the intellect stimulated?

How much is knowledge and personal discovery encouraged?

How much are skills and competencies being formed?

How much models are presented and interacted with?

How much is talent assertion being encouraged?

How much is the education personalized?

To what extent is work and discipline encouraged?

How is character developed?

How holistic is the education process?

How relevant is the current approach for the student? What about for society?

What should be the main criteria for evaluating a quality educational system?

What current issues get too little importance and what current issues get too much?

What structural system changes should be made?

How relevant is the annual curriculum?

What are the related activities that have to do with education?

How accessible are these to children?

What are the things that undermine the learning process?

How are the local community and business environments involved in facilitating children's education?

How developed is the infrastructure in the educational system?

How much is innovation encouraged in education? With what mentality? What stakes? With what risks? After which model, theoretical or practical? With what results?

What are the most suitable performance indicators?

How do they apply objectively and according to the specifics of each student?

Which performance indicators can be combined with others, and which not?

What are the evaluation criteria? How are the results being quantified? How to combine different indicators?

To what extent does the teacher's feedback motivate the student towards performance?

What would a more constructive competition between students look like? What about between teachers?

How early could the students' natural inclinations be identified? How could they be stimulated and supported?

What would be the most appropriate approach for rural education?

How could education be adapted to students' personality and preferences?

How could the student be exposed to more opportunities and learning methods?

How could education be better applied and more imaginative?

What is the most appropriate stage in the child's life for more abstract notions?

What is the age at which it is normal for students to receive generalized education? When should specialization elements be added to the student? Depending on what factors (age, etc.) is the proportion of general and special education established?

What helps (different) children to supplement their efforts to learn?

How could coaching be facilitated in the lives of the pupils and students, at least in the key period decisions?

How could students at the university grow helped by mentors?

How can students benefit from more financial support?

What would encourage students to be more self-taught?

What opportunities for informal or non-formal education would make a significant difference?

How much is the character of pupils and students formed?

How are teachers encouraged to improve their teaching and perform better?

What are the main entities in the field of education?

What job would you prefer? What is the role you are targeting?

What do you really think you should do? What are you going to do?

Media

If you were to run the entire media field in your country, what measures would you take immediately? What are your criteria for setting priorities? What should you keep in mind?

What would your priorities be?

What are the main media needs at national level? What about those at the local level?

What type of media has the greatest impact?

What are the main media entities? What are their specifics? What are their strengths? What are the criteria for assessing a media entity?

What is the main role of the media? What about the next one?

What is the potential for positive impact of media? What should happen so that it becomes reality?

What are the most negative media effects? For whom? Through what? How could they be diminished? What are the underlying causes?

What should be the values of media that fulfills its purpose with excellence?

How much is the definition of truth influenced? How much is the reality distorted? How much manipulation is there?

How much is the individual's freedom respected to be informed and think for himself?

What do you think is the most genuine alternative to how the current media informs and influences the audience?

How do you think the media will look like over a certain number of years?

What factors play an important role? What factors will diminish their importance?

What are the trends?

What role does technology play?

What are the main types of audiences? What about subtypes? What are their preferences? What is the representative profile for each category? What are the most significant audiences? According to what criteria?

What are the factors that slow down development?

What is the potential for development? What are the opportunities?

What are the main media entities?

If the future of the media could look very different because of you, what great change would you like to initiate?

What job would you prefer? What role are you targeting?

> *What do you really think you should do? What are you going to do?*

Environment

If you become the new Minister of the Environment, what would be the most significant measures you would take?

What are your criteria for prioritizing? What should you keep in mind?

What would your priorities be?

What problems have been neglected globally so far? What about at national level? What about at a local level?

What changes would you introduce?

What are the main environmental approaches?

What is your perspective on the relationship between the environment and man?

What do you think is the fundamental reason why man should be environmentally friendly?

What is the role of the environment in relation to man?

In what ways can the environment be a blessing to man? Under what conditions?

In what ways can the environment be unfavorable to man? Under what conditions?

What is the role of man in relation to the environment? What do you think are the responsibilities of humanity towards the environment?

What are the main environmental problems? With what implications? To what extent is the man responsible for these?

What do you think are the main causes of environmental problems? What about the most fundamental problem?

What are the factors on which man has no control in relation to the environment? How could man have control? With what benefits? At what risk?

What do you really think you should do? What are you going to do?

Families

If you were the authority that has the greatest influence on the families in your country, what measures would you immediately take? What are other decision makers that you should collaborate with?

What would be your criteria for prioritizing? What things should you keep in mind?

What would your priorities be?

How do you see the family institution?

What do you think is its role in society?

What is your ideal family?

What is the theoretical model you wish to be transposed into reality?

What are the challenges of contemporary families?

What are the current needs?

What are the trends?

What are the opportunities?

How could the relationships between spouses be improved? What are the most critical issues? What is neglected in reality? Why?

How could the relationships between parents and children be improved? What are the most significant aspects? What could be done in a concrete way?

How could children be better cared for?

How could children be better educated?

What would a truly favorable environment for family relationships look like?

How could children receive more love and support?

What threatens the contemporary family? What about spouses? What about the children?

What good things should be maximized? What excesses should be limited?

> *What do you really think you should do? What are you going to do?*

Governance/Politics

What is the identity of the largest group you want to represent? What is its history? What are its heroes? What are its values?

What are its interests?

What smaller group are you resonating with the most? What are the characteristics that define it?

How could you position yourself for the best in the favor of as many people as possible?

How would you define politics in your own words? What do you understand by political involvement? Which are the main political actions of an ordinary citizen? When is someone apolitical?

What is your political philosophy? What are the values that should underpin good governance? What is the role of the state in society? How do you see the relationship between authorities and private individuals? What about the relationship between state and private institutions?

When is a society free?

How important is the rule of law?

What should be the boundaries of political power?

What is the role of self-government?

How important is the ability of the governors to make moral decisions?

How would you characterize the current political class?

What are your role models of political leaders? What do you appreciate about them?

Which political group do you identify with the most?

How likely are you to initiate one?

How could you be more selfless to the public benefit?

How could you act with more determination in the right direction?

What are the main problems you want fixed?

What are your long-term priorities?

What are your main challenges?

What should happen for you to persevere?

Which of the following two positions characterizes the majority? "Because of the current political situation I don't think I should really get involve", or " because of the current political situation I think I should really get involve "? What about you personally?

> *What do you really think you should do? What are you going to do?*

Health

As the new Minister of Health, what would be the most important measures you would take?

What are your criteria for prioritizing? What should you keep in mind?

What would your priorities be?

What are the main approaches to health? Which are the most significant differences? Who are the representatives of the main approaches?

What areas of health need to be reformed the most?

What do you think are the strategic pillars for a healthy health system?

How important is prevention? How is this reflected into practice?

What role does the insurance system play? How could it be improved?

How important is management in the health system? How could it be improved?

What are the main problems at national level? What about locally?

What would be the best long-term solutions?

What are the categories of people who have specific health needs?

What is the innovation potential of the domain that concerns you?

What are the trends? What is society evolving towards in terms of health?

What are the main challenges in the present? What do you think these will be over a certain number of years?

What do you think are the factors that will play a more important role?

What areas or issues are left behind?

What are the opportunities?

How could resources and skills be combined for more impact?

What do you think the strategic priorities for health should be?

What are the areas related to the health system?

What are the main entities in the health system?

What job would you prefer? What is the role you are targeting?

> *What do you really think you should do? What are you going to do?*

Justice

What measures would you take first and foremost if you had just been appointed as Minister of Justice?

What would be your criteria for setting priorities? What should you take into account?

What would your priorities be?

What are the roles of justice?

What are the main pillars in the justice system?

What type of job would you prefer? What is the position you are aiming for?

What are your strengths to activate in this line of work?

What kind of situations do you think would make the most of your strengths? What would challenge you to evolve in your career?

What are the main problems of the justice system?

In what field or specific issue is there urgent need for innovation?

What are the issues that are left behind?

Who are the key people in justice? What are their strengths, what about their limits?

What are the main component categories of the justice system?

What are the main types of illegalities?

Without discriminating, what are the categories of people more prone to committing illegalities? What are the determining factors?

Who are the most vulnerable people to become victims?

What are the determining factors?

What are the trends? What are the factors that matter the most?

What are the opportunities?

What legislative changes do you think are necessary?

> *What do you really think you should do? What are you going to do?*

Art

What would this country look like if all people loved art as much as you? What would the main differences be?

What are the reasons why some people do not give sufficient importance to art?

Why should more people be concerned about art?

Which artistic expression is the most popular? Why is that so?

What are the main artistic forms that are underestimated?

What are the current tendencies in art?

What is your favorite field of art? Why are you more prone to this field?

What are your goals and objectives for this field?

What potential do you think has not been explored enough yet? Why is that?

What is the niche you would like to focus on? What are its most representative qualities?

What are the most noteworthy challenges?

What should happen to overcome them?

What responsibilities do you take for this?

> *What do you really think you should do? What are you going to do?*

Sport

What are the reasons you love sports?

What are the strengths of a man who is passionate about sports?

How would you motivate a young person to practise a certain sport?

If you became the Minister of Sport, what would be the first measures you would take?

What main skills do you think a sports teacher should have? What about a coach?

What is the local sport that attracts most fans? Why is that? To what extent do the following factors matter?

> The personal experience in that sport?
>
> Local popularity and waves that also include others?
>
> Top athletes who have become "idols" and inspire others?
>
> Media exposure?
>
> Inherited tradition?
>
> Financing education?
>
> Infrastructure and within the means facilities?
>
> What other factors?

What are other sports that have the potential to become equally popular? What should happen for this to take place? What would a strategic plan look like for the next 10 years? How likely it is to become a reality?

What are the more (maybe) niche types of sports, but which offer unique privileges for a particular type of athletes and fans? To what extent do the following opportunities (and challenges at the same time) matter?

> Belonging to a group with the same passion?
>
> Elite entourage?
>
> Is local competition currently at a low point?
>
> External journeys and cross-cultural interaction?

> *To pioneer and innovate,*

Which sport practiced in other countries, would you like to develop in your country as well?
What new sports could you create?
What sports could be combined to develop a new one?
What are the strengths of the most popular sports that could be concentrated in the sport you want to develop?
What if you focused almost exclusively on discovering and promoting new talents?

What do you really think you should do?
What are you going to do?

4.2. THINKING RICH AND ALTRUISTIC [1]

What are the categories of people you could significantly help without necessarily resorting to material resources?

How could you help others to raise awareness of their inner potential? What about being more positive, more hopeful?

How could you help others see opportunities?

How could you stimulate people's creativity?

How could you be a source of inspiration and encouragement to others?

How could you help those who have low self-esteem or identity problems?

How could you assert the importance and intrinsic value of those who do not believe in it, or underestimate it?

How could you help the poverty-stricken people to self-sustain themselves? How could you empower them to do the same for others?

How could you compensate for the lack of education in the lives of others? What about the lack of accomplishments or possessions?

What are the main causes of poverty in your vicinity?

How could you fight them on a long-term? In the first place?

How could you help those who are aware of their potential to create wealth, and value it?

How could you influence people to be more altruistic, and more empathic with those in need?

How can you spark the wealthiest to want to help more those in need? How could you help those who already want it, or need some support to manifest their actions? What about those who already invest in others, how could you help them make it in a more strategic way in the long run?

What kind of support would you like to give?

What are the causes that attract you to get involved?

How could you help others to put their abilities at work in order to create and multiply wealth, and reduce poverty around them?

How could you motivate others to overcome their own limitations?

How could you inspire people's thoughts in order for them to better manage their relationships, roles, responsibilities and resources?

How could you trigger people to cherish quality and aesthetics more? What about having high aspirations?

How could you inspire the faith of people around you? For whom in the first place?

How could you notice and encourage certain special abilities of others?

How could you help people to better relate to failure and suffering? How about managing their risks? What about coping with criticism and resolving conflicts?

How could you help people make the most of their time?

How could you train people in certain areas where they are already outstanding, or where they are deficient?

How could you stimulate the development of the emotional intelligence of those around you?

4.3. UNDERSTANDING THE NEEDS[2]

What concrete needs in society are you currently concerned about? What about those concerning your field of interest? What about another field?

To what do you have the greatest curiosity and pursuit at present? How determined are you to bring a remarkable improvement?

What is it that you feel most responsible for? Towards who?

What are the problems that no one seems to be looking for true solutions or more effective solutions? What about those that are most completely ignored by the majority?

What unfulfilled needs do you want to connect with innovation and development opportunities?

What comes naturally to you when you effortlessly and constantly observe around you?

What is the problem for which you are willing to invest the most to have it fixed?

In what field do you think you are most likely to succeed in connecting the necessary with the possible? What is supposed to happen? What are you supposed to do?

In what area or specific aspect do you strive to reach a better approach, to a more effective method?

What role does empathy play in the area that concerns you? How could you make the most of your empathy?

What immediate needs threaten your focus on real needs? By what concrete measures could you persevere?

What kind of adaptations would be beneficial to respond to important needs? What should be implemented? How?

What need of the society has drawn your attention in particular? What could you do about it? What are you supposed to do? What are you going to do?

4.4. CHALLENGING THE STATUS-QUO[3]

In what area of society are you most prone to think and act out of the box?

What do you think is the most outdated sector?

In what situation are you inclined to go against the tide?

What aspect of your field of interest do you feel is nonetheless erroneous or disadvantageous although generally accepted?

What rooted idea frustrates you? What about the customs, or traditions?

What method is outdated?

Towards what do you hold the most positive skepticism?

What popular belief are you determined to challenge? How widespread are these? With what effects?

What area or appearance do you think has the greatest reformation potential? What issue do you think should be revolutionized?

What assertions do you feel to be erroneous?

What fragility do you perceive in the building foundation?

What activism could be redirected?

In what field or aspect are you an intuitive nonconformist?

Where could you support the unconventional? With whom would you be able to take action? What about testing? What about associating? To what limits?

How do you put your critical thinking into practice in a constructive way? What is the ideal context?

4.5. CAPITALIZING ON TRENDS[4]

What are the current trends in your area of concern? What about the connected ones? What international trends do you feel will reach your context? Conversely, what local trend could go global?

Towards what is it most likely to have current trends converge on? With what impact? What kind of turning points could make a great difference? What disruptive factors deserve more attention?

What big change can you catch sight of? How likely is it for you to be the pioneer and the driving force of that change? What would be your element of originality: a new style, a new technique, a new discovery, a new method, a new form, a new system, a new type of...?

What is the current trend that is the least noticed? Which qualitative or quantitative leap would it favor? What are the factors that point to a great potential movement?

What trend in the present is waiting for you to make a big difference in the long run? How can you maximize your resourcefulness, creativity and inventiveness?

What is the most widespread trend? How does it affect you? How could you use this trend as a springboard, or as a vehicle? What about the most unnoticed? Due to which factors?

If you analyzed the most relevant trends, what are they converging on?

What are the fundamental changes that occur in the environment in which you engage? How well do you understand them?

How much effort are you willing to put in to revitalize or reinvent your way of working?

4.5. CONNECTING OPPORTUNITIES[5]

What are your most noteworthy assets and abilities? How could these be recombined to give rise to new opportunities? In what context?

What are your strengths that might help you in a different context?

What could you adapt to a new project for greater impact than the previous one? What could be the most strategic connections to succeed?

What opportunities in another field could you use in your field to innovate and create?

What is your skills portfolio? What could you possibly be channeling them into? What skills would you like to develop in the first place?

How could you encourage those around you to build on their unlimited capacity for developing, expanding, combining and channeling resources? How do you develop such a culture in a team or every department in the organization?

How about watching the group of departments in your organization as a portfolio of basic skills and strategic assets? How could you combine and channel them in new ways to generate innovation and development?

How could you revolutionize your domain by combining internal and external resources? Who would you go into partnership with? What about in a different kind of relationship?

5. VISION

*what image of the future
energizes you?*

5.1. VISION, MISSION, STRATEGY, AND VALUES

What is the meaning of these terms?

Vision

What is the exhilarating image of the future? How do you imagine your future after the implementation of your dream? What would help you establish a clear vision?

Mission

What is the organization going to do as a purpose of its existence? What is the essence of your involvement so that the vision becomes reality? What is your main contribution to society/humanity? What is the ultimate objective at which all others will contribute? What will be the point of other activities?

Strategy

How will the mission translate into practice? Through what? What are the most important objectives, priorities, goals and tactical activities you will undertake to accomplish your mission?

What difference can a precise mission statement make for you and your organization?

Values

What is the core identity of the organization in relation to the purpose for which it exists? What makes it so special? What makes it sustainable? How do you want the organization to be over the years, as an expression of these values? What reputation do you want it to have? What if these values actually embody the DNA of your organization?

5.2. IMPRESSIONS FROM THE FUTURE

Exploration, clarification, motivation, challenge, and relevance

What is the ideal you dream of?

What is that purpose of yours, which is so outstanding that you are ready to do everything you can to accomplish it in this life?

What is your idea of the future viewed as eccentric or insane by the more practical or more conformist people?

How do your aspirations disturb the people around you? Who will your visionary initiatives disrupt in the first place? In what way?

Who will be blessed by your visionary initiatives? In what way?

If that 1% of Thomas Edison's success formula were the foundation for what you are called to accomplish in life, what would be that 1%?

What if this foundation were your very vision, how would you formulate it?

If you already saw your vision accomplished, how would you feel? What would be your greatest fulfilment? If you had a regret, what would that be?

If you were to present your vision to some first grade students, what would you tell them?

What if you should present your vision to potential investors?

What if you had to present your vision to some dying men?

The Imagined Impact

For how many people do you estimate that achieving your vision will have a significant impact?

Who are those people in the first place?

In what ways will it have an impact on them?

What about the other categories of people affected?

How could you maximize the impact?

What is your vision? What is the image you visualize when you think about the future? What image of the future do you want to focus your energy on?

How much are you passionate about it?

How much time do you think it will take for your vision to become reality?

What difference do you expect your vision to make when it comes true?

How do you imagine the future in 10 years? What about 50?

What do you most passionate about when you think about fulfilling your vision?

What are the areas that will be reconciled?

Who will be the people who will benefit the most?

What are the five most important aspects of your vision?

If you had to describe your vision in five words, what would those be?

What is the maximum potential of this vision?

What would make another visionary want to join your vision?

Who would your enthusiasm touch?

Why do you think your model could be a great encouragement to other visionaries?

How do you act when you do not share the new vision of a leader you already follow?

[Stages In] Clarification Of Vision

Why would you want more clarity?

When does a vision seem too broad to you? When is it too narrow?

What extreme would you avoid in the first place? What impact would it have on you if you didn't avoid that extreme?

What does a well-defined vision look like to you?

What are the critical elements of a vision?

What are the advantages for a clearly defined vision? What about the dangers?

What are the fundamentals of vision that could be defined more specifically?

If you should estimate how long it will take to see your vision come true, what would be the minimum time? What about the maximum? What about the most reasonable?

How would you formulate this vision if you only had half the estimated time available? (How do you imagine the future in half of the initial estimated time?)

If you should express your vision in a minimum number of words, what would those words be?

What if you should present it to an ideal audience?

Motivation To Persevere In Achieving The Vision

What exactly motivates you the most about this vision?

What makes you think that this vision is not just a beautiful dream, or a mere desire?

How could you increase the sense of ownership of the vision?

What should happen for the vision to stir more enthusiasm and energy for someone in particular?

What are the main reasons why a certain person could reach the point of embracing the vision?

What influence would it have if the vision became reality over a certain number of years? What about along the way, if that person should join the vision, wholeheartedly?

If The Vision Were A Puzzle

What would be the most representative pieces to see the big picture?

What would be the rest of the pieces that make up the overall picture?

How do you find their number (from the overall picture, before you notice that each piece can be another puzzle itself)?

What would be the most essential piece?

If you should choose the pieces in order of their importance, what would the order be?

How long do you estimated that this puzzle will be a faithful depiction of a fulfilled future?

If you had to divide this period into several stages, and then give them names, what would they be?

If you should choose the pieces in chronological order (for accomplishment), what would be the order? How would you order them in relation to the above steps?

As the owner of the vision

What do you think is the most strategic piece to fit?

What is your favorite piece? When do you think it will be fitted?

What about the piece you want to avoid? Why is that?

What is the piece you need a miracle for? What kind of miracle?

What are the key factors for the success of this puzzle?

Challenge Of Vision, Importance And Relevance

If you were a simple member of your team, what would a set vision help you with? What difference would this make in your daily work?

What are the first three reasons why someone would want to join your vision?

In maximum three words, which is for you the most appropriate expression, when you think about vision? What about in one word?

Imagine yourself old, telling your grandchildren the realization of the vision, what would be the key point of the story? If a nephew asked you what was your inner motivation that has never faded, what would you say to him?

For what unique responsibility do you have the impression that you were entrusted with by the divinity?

5.3. COMMUNICATING THE VISION

How could you communicate better, to have a greater impact, to inspire, to transmit, to involve, to energize, or to (re)focus?

Strategic Communication

What is the audience that would be happy to know your vision?

What is the audience that is already interested in what you have to offer?

What is the audience that is not interested in yet, but is likely to become?

How do you think they prefer you communicate with them?

Communication Context

Who do you want to communicate to?

What is the purpose for which you want to communicate?

What are you going to have to focus on?

How would you like to communicate? How could you be more

creative? What about more interesting? How about to express yourself naturally and passionately?

What is the audience that would naturally be the most receptive and enthusiastic about this vision?

The Story Of Your Own Vision

What preceded this vision?

What were your thoughts about the state of the matter before the current vision? What feelings were you experiencing?

How did you end up having this vision, or how did it come to you?

How did you feel then?

What has contributed to the development of the vision so far?

To what extent have other people contributed to shaping the vision?

What impact did it have on you? What has changed in your way of thinking and acting?

What were your minimum and maximum moments concerning the vision you received?

6. COMMON IDENTITY

what are your specific?

Before you offer your dream product or service, who are you really? What does your DNA consist of? What qualities are essential for you to succeed in the long run? What defines the culture of your organization? By what unique combination of values and principles will you differentiate yourself from other entities and your competition?

What is the value towards which you want your organization to advance, beyond the products or services you will offer?

As you grow, beyond the profit, what will give a sense to your achievements? What will be most significant?

6.1. VALUES

If your organization were a laptop, what would be your antivirus? That do you estimate as main threats to your integrity and existence? How do you ensure the optimal functioning of the antivirus?

What are the fundamental values of your team? In what order?

What are your ethical standards?

What is your position on corruption? But what about materialism, greed and selfishness?

How do you maintain integrity and kindness?

How do you protect your freedom in the long run? What about people's dignity?

How will you contribute to more justice and peace in the company and society?

How will you affect disadvantaged people?

How will you protect the environment?

How will you convey the truth? How will you shape honesty?

What social problem will you solve or prevent?

How will you cherish innovation?

How important is the quality you offer?

How much does the quality of team relationships matter? What about the relationship with your beneficiaries? What other relationships are very important?

By what will you gain or build authority, respect and a place in history?

6.2. GUIDELINES

Although setting these is not necessarily the strong point of visionary leaders, they can be of strategic importance for key situations and habits that affect the future of the organization or company, and can protect freedom from sustainable development.

What are the internal principles that will help you transpose the assumed values into practice?

What are the areas that should not escape the implementation of the above values? What are the basic criteria? What are the key aspects?

How could they be formulated positively and friendly, but in a clear and firm manner? How about more creatively? How about more artistically? Where you might add some humor?

How could they be more easily remembered? How about lower in number?

How could these be less focused on behavior and more on an internal superior motivation?

How are they modeled by the people in the management?

What do they transmit to visitors, for interns or for the beneficiaries of your work?

6.3. BRAND

How would you like to be perceived by the public? What about employees? What about customers? What about the competition? What about society?

In what field do you want to excel? For who? Through what?

What concept best reflects your identity?

What defines you best? What are the specific elements that should be highlighted?

Who should your brand be most relevant to?

How would you like to represent this graphically? How about in a more relevant way? How about in a more elegant, or simpler way? How about in a more suggestive way?

What do you want your logo to convey?

Who can you consult with for the most appropriate choices?

How much do you want to be online? What about other areas in the media?

Which social networks are the most used by your target group?

7. MISSION

what actions will you essentially undertake?

7.1. THE MEANING OF THE MISSION

What is the organization going to do, as the purpose of its existence?
What is the essence of your involvement so that the vision becomes a reality?
What is the purpose of your organization?
What is your main contribution to society/humanity?
What is the ultimate objective to which all the others will contribute?
What will be the purpose of other activities?

If the vision is the destination to which you are heading for, what is essentially the activity you perform to get there?

What is the action that subordinates all others?

What should the joint effort converge on?

What is your greatest responsibility publicly assumed?

What do you want to offer the others, through everything you do inside the movement?

What is the spearhead of all your actions?

What is the ultimate criterion by which you evaluate your entire activity?

Finally, what is your basic assignment?

> *What is your personal life mission? To what extent does it match that of the organization?*

> *For what unique responsibility do you have the impression that you were entrusted with by the divinity?*

7.2. THE PURPOSE OF THE MISSION

What would help you as a visionary leader to have a clearly defined mission?
What about the team members?
What about the target audience?
What would happen if you didn't have a clear mission?
What difference would it make in everyday activity?
Who is your mission most relevant to? Who else?

What difference can a mission make when it is publicly assumed?

7.3. THE ELABORATION OF THE MISSION STATEMENT

What are the five main words in the mission statement?
What do you want to put the accent on?
What is the main verb in this statement?
How many options have you analyzed to reach this conclusion?
For whom is the mission statement in the first place?
How relevant is it?
Who did you consult with?
What about people outside the organization?
What feedback have you received so far?
How could you formulate it more accurately and more concisely?
How about more easily remembered?
How often or how rare should it be reviewed and updated?

7.4. COMMUNICATING THE MISSION

Who would benefit from finding out about your organization's mission? Who would be the first? What would you like to be the impact of the vision communication?

What are the risks of poor communication?

How could you maximize the communication impact?

What are the possible obstacles on the receiver's side?

What resonates with him? How could you come across the obstacles?

What should you do to improve your communication mode? What should you keep in mind? What would be the best way of communicating? How could you do that as creatively as possible?

Who has the greatest need to remember your mission statement?

How often do you think it would help to be reheard or revised?

How do you make sure it won't be forgotten? Or ignored? Or trivialized? Or discredited?

How about making sure it will be applied with responsibility and faithfulness?

Who are you preparing to communicate to?

In what context?
For what purpose?
What is the specific of the audience?
What do you want to put the accent on?
How do you make the introduction?
What about the conclusion?

PART II - FOR IMPLEMENTATION

Strategy, Team, and Resources

8. STRATEGY

what does the master plan look like?

How will the mission translate into practice? Through what?

What are the most important objectives, priorities, goals and tactical activities you will undertake to accomplish your mission?

What practical difference can the precise formulation of a mission statement make for you and your organization?

8.1. PLANNING THE JOURNEY TO YOUR DESTINATION

Where are you going?

How useful is the journey?

What about friends who joined the adventure? Or for those you will meet at your destination?

What is the ideal route?

What are the travel conditions?

How far have we gotten since we started?

Who am I traveling with?

Who else do you want to make happy on this journey? Who is helpful?

How does the team feel?

What cars are you traveling with? What is their technical status? What comfort do they offer?

With what average speed will you travel? How does this translate into the estimated time of arrival?

What are the planned stops? What other stops do you need? Or the justifiable ones?

How could you prevent damage?

Where do you put gas from? What quality?

What are the costs? How do you cover them?

8.2. STRATEGIC PRIORITIES

How useful can actions that are not connected to a well thought out general plan be?

Before there is anything urgent to do, what would be the most important thing to do? How likely is it to be just compiling a strategy?

What would the scheme that includes the most important long-term goals look like? How would you represent it graphically?

What is the most strategic thing you have accomplished so far?

What is the most strategic thing you are currently pursuing?

What do you think will be the next most strategic thing you want to accomplish?

What are the factors that determine your priorities?

What are the priorities in your personal life?

How do you adjust your priorities to the current season?

How do you make sure you respect your priorities?

How do you assess compliance with priorities?

What are the most common threats to your priorities?

What are the really important things for you?

To what extent the priorities set help you focus on the really important things?

What do you think of the following statement: The real priorities are revealed when you look behind you?

What is the most difficult part in maintaining a priority?

How do you make sure you transpose your priorities into practice?

From the experience you have gained so far, what are the main lurking time thieves?

How do you know when you have respected your priority ? What are the evaluation indicators?

Personally or in a team, which behavior best reflects that priority?

How do you celebrate (reward) keepng a priority at the end of a specific period?

Focus And Optimization

How important is the focus for you? How much would that help?

If you were to do one thing, with excellence, what would that be?

What is your main enemy keeping you from focusing?

What is your main concern at present? What would you like it to be? What is it going to be?

To what extent do urgent things hold you back from important things?

What is the most important change you would like to take up? What about the next?

How often do you think structural changes can be needed? How about in the way of work? What about in technology? What about working conditions? What about leadership? What about other people involved? What about of other type?

What is that change, which if you took up you would solve several problems simultaneously?

What is the main criterion after which you establish your priorities? What about the next one?

What are the most important indicators of growth and development?

Convergence And Refocusing

How important is it for you to align all the elements of the organization with the established vision?

How easy is it for you to stay focused in pursuing your vision?

What are the factors that threaten your attention and focus?

What helps you to (re)focus?

What is the mechanism / tactic by which you could make sure that all elements of the organization are properly aligned?

By what do you want to stimulate team members to remain loyal to your mission?

What are the possible distractions for the team?

What team members show the most dedication? What are the key factors in their case?

What team members have divergent tendencies? What factors influence their behavior?

8.3. OBJECTIVES, GOALS AND TACTICAL ACTIONS

Ambitions Test

What is the source of your ambitions?

What impact do your ambitions have on the team? (Overwhelming, exhaustion, inspiration, challenge, etc.)

How much would it affect you if someone else would get appreciation for a job well done under your leadership?

How do you perceive the successes of other leaders (threat, inspiration, etc.)?

Objectives

What are the most important goals for a certain period of time?

How are these related to strategic priorities?

How does the achievement of a specific objective contribute to the fulfillment of the mission and the realization of the vision?

What if for each objective a mission statement was formulated?

What would a graphical representation look like with the main objectives in relation to the mission and vision?

How does the achievement of some goals depend on others?

Smart Goals

How could you plan to achieve each main goal with smaller, well-defined goals?

How could that aim be as specific as possible?

How do you know it is completed well?

By which measurable indicators?

How achievable (not just bold) is the intended purpose?

How much does it matter to be accomplished? Why is it important?

What is the deadline for the accomplishment?

How do you develop a culture driven by intentional goals, accomplished with ambition and success? What about with more satisfaction and less stress?

Strategy Implementation Tactics

How slow, in the absence of appropriate actions to the strategy, would be your route to the next victory?

Specifically, how do you choose the most appropriate moves for the present?

What are the particulars of that context? What are the factors that can hinder success? What about those that can favor it?

How could you do the best in a certain situation?

To meet a strategic plan, what kind of tactical actions are

needed? What are those exact actions that have the greatest potential to infer upon short-term results?

What are the most likely scenarios along the way?

At a certain point in time, what could be the best decision?

What is more natural to you: to design a strategic plan, or, based on it, to realize what are the most appropriate tactical actions?

What should happen in order to succeed in having both a good strategic plan and good tactical actions? Who could help you?

How much do you care about preparing to achieve your goals with maximum efficiency? How important is it to give time for study, analysis and organization for maximum impact? What about time to put everything into practice?

How well do you think that you master the science of determining, for a short period, the conduct of a movement adapted to the respective circumstances, to achieve a fundamental objective?

What period does your strategy cover? What do you think will be the most important moments? In what order? What tactical actions should be undertaken before each important moment? What about before this?

What adjustments could make the difference to success?

Accountability

How important is it for you to work with responsible people? What about you being a role model?

How do you encourage, facilitate or ensure responsibility for those involved?

What would help the most, objectively? What side effects could it produce?

How could you test the impact on those affected?

What concrete actions could you undertake for this? How could you communicate best?

8.4. STAGES AND DEADLINES

How should progress be reflected on the timeline?

Stages

What would the mission statement look like if divided over a certain number of years?

What would be the main stages in development, in order to achieve the highest objectives?

What is the specifics of each stage? What is the most appropriate name for each?

How about customizing the mission statement for each step, specifically?

How should the strategic plan for each stage look like? What should it contain?

Deadlines

How realistic are the deadlines? How daring are they?

What should you make sure happens to progress at a promising pace? What is it, first and foremost?

What are the advantages of respecting the deadlines? Who does it depend on?

What are the consequences of non-compliance with deadlines? Who does it affect?

What indicators enable progress to be measured? How could these be more clearly defined? What about easier to supervise?

8.5. TESTS: PERSEVERANCE AND RESULTS

Perseverance Test

If Thomas Edison grants success a percentage of 99% for perspiration, how do you see the inspiration-effort ratio?

What does perseverance mean to you?

What are things or situations where it is natural for you to be perseverant?

What motivates you most to be persevering?

What are the things or situations in which you tend to have difficulty persevering?

What helps you persevere when you experience difficulties?

If a great-grandson of yours asks you what made you persevere to succeed, what would you say?

Test Results

How much does it matter that the activity carried out produces the expected results?

How are productivity and efficiency measured? By what indicators?

When do performance indicators indicate excellence? When do they communicate growth potential? What about temporary failure? Or bankruptcy?

What are the indicators for different levels of risk?

When is it necessary to increase expectations? What about tempering ambitions?

When are efficiency adjustments required? When would these be counter-productive?

How much is the whole affected by some seemingly minor deficiencies?

When are radical changes required?

9. THE TEAM

with whom do you progress?

9.1. PEOPLE AND ROLES

How important is the team for you with whom you see the vision becoming a reality?

What Are The Selection Criteria For Team Members?

What would you like your team to stand out compared to other teams? With what stake?

How open are they in collaboration with the other team members?

How agreeable are they (with you and others)?

How competent are they for those responsibilities? What potential do you see in them?

How compatible are their values with the team values?

How courageous are they to act under pressure guided by faith?

How capable are they to manage their feelings in situations of pressure and risk in leadership?

To what extent are they ready to work in a cultural diversity?

Personality, Skills And Endowments

What is the specificity of the job that you want to entrust to someone?

What is the ideal person for this? What personal qualities should they have? What about skills?

What is the type of personality that best matches the role or responsibility required within the team?

What are the natural talents needed? What about the ones that can be acquired along the way? What opportunities do you offer for this?

What is the personality profile of the ideal person? What about the spiritual one?

How much does it matter for the person to have a sense of calling and purpose to be part of the team, for a specific role?

What are the expectations that must necessarily be communicated by you? What about the other party?

The Trust Factor

How reliable are team people or how reliable should they be?

What are the people in the team who give you the utmost confidence? How do you repay their trust?

What are the factors that retain others from giving you more trust?

How could you develop a climate of trust?

Motivate

How do you stimulate the sense of ownership for team members? Or the feeling of belonging?

How do you communicate appreciation to team members for their specific contribution? How often? How authentically?

How do you boost the efficiency of team members? How do you measure it? What are the objectives that need to be met? How clear and realistic are they? How ambitious?

Rewards

How do you reward the efficiency of team members?

How appropriate is this in relation to the performance target? How about in relation to their efforts?

How are the rewards perceived by the team members? What is the real impact of the rewards?

What could be improved? What other creative rewards could you offer?

How often do you state the achievements of a team member or the whole team?

What is the best way to motivate a particular team member

How could you develop a team competition that is both constructive and entertaining?

Loyalty[31]

Is it more natural for team members to be loyal to leaders or the organization?

On a scale of 1 to 10, how loyal are team members to the common vision?

Who are the people closest to the maximum? Who do you think should become more loyal?

How do you maintain a strong interest in your team for the organization's vision?

What are the risks of poor loyalty?

What about an unhealthy loyalty? What situations should be avoided?

What are the factors that motivate them to follow you?

How much transparency is practised in the working environment?

How do you promote an atmosphere of mutual trust?

How do you encourage sincere dialogue and feedback, or even disagreement?

To what extent is your team's loyalty rewarded?

What could threaten their loyalty?

What is up to you to boost their loyalty?

What are the challenges of team members that are true tests of loyalty.

To what extent do you offer the same loyalty you expect from them?

Stability And Change

As you lead people toward change, what do you do to ensure them minimal stability?

What are the people who naturally prefer stability? What about those who embrace change?

What is the most suitable combination for the anticipated development?

9.2. THE ETHOS OF THE TEAM

Team Ethos

How would you describe the team in three words?

How would you characterize the team mentality? What could improve? How?

How much is the team's attitude approaching "is it possible, and we will do all that is up to us to succeed"?

What is the predominant mood of the team?

How selfless is the team as a whole? What are the most remarkable acts of altruism?

9.3. WORKING ATMOSPHERE

What are the most positive aspects about your team? What team members are you most pleased with? Who needs more attention or support?

How do you distinguish any personal shortcomings of team members?

What are the possible hidden issues that would require a discerning approach?

Trust

How do you cultivate trust in your team?

What are the vulnerabilities within the team?

What are the threats to an environment full of trust?

Unity

How united is your team?

What does a truly united team look like to you?

What are the things that reflect the unity?

How unitary does the team act?

Where are any shortcomings of coordination, interaction or communication?

What would a higher quality team building look like?

Respect

What is your favorite way of showing respect to your team?

But how about their way of feeling respected?

What about the recipients of your work?

9.4. NETWORKING

What are the people you would like to connect with? For what? Where are they?

What are the people who have similar interests to yours? Where would you meet them? Do you see them as potential partners or your competition?

What could you offer them? How could they help you? Why whoul they be interested?

Who are the people you think are naturally most interested in what you have to offer?

How could you interact with them?

9.5. LEADERSHIP, DEVELOPMENT, AND CARE[32]

Leadership

How clear is for each member the direction in which the team should head?

How good is coordination at every level of the organization? What doesn't work properly? How could this be improved?

How motivated is the team to accomplish their mission with passion and excellence? What would make a significant improvement?

How well does the leadership work?

How much do you invest in leadership development?

What are the aspects in which the current leadership limits growth? What kind of help does it need?

Who would you get more involved in the leadership?

Development

How much are you concerned about team development? How natural is it to you? Who could help you?

9.5. LEADERSHIP, DEVELOPMENT, AND CARE[32]

What are the areas in which the team should necessarily develop?

How could you assess the team for a more appropriate knowledge of development needs?

What impact would the team for a more adequate knowledge of the development needs?

What are the most appropriate development opportunities? How do you know that?

Who are the key people whose development would be worth investing in as a priority? How open are they for a path you have planned?

What are the regular opportunities for continuous development?

How effective are the opportunities or development programs so far?

What kind of courses, seminars, conferences or workshops could you facilitate for team members?

What could you teach your team?

Who do you offer coaching to?

In whom do you invest in a particular way through mentoring?

What kind of resources could you make available to the team for further development?

When will the next quality team building take place?

How could you facilitate and encourage desired development opportunities or even initiated by team members?

In addition to the qualitative growth of the team members, how can you enlarge your team, and implicitly the ability to fulfill your mission?

What are the strategic elements for this?

Care

How would the team act if each member would be treated with more care? How would everyone feel knowing that you really care about him/her as a person, beyond the contribution to the achievement of the objectives?

If you considered your team members as friends, how would you relate to them? What would be different? What if you were their older brother or even their parent?

How could you show more empathy towards the team members? What would this look like in practice?

In the current context, who needs extra attention, understanding or support?

How could the team's well-being increase?

Why else do team members need to work to their full potential?

Celebrate

What is the impact of the celebration on the team? How do team members feel when attending a celebration? What does this communicate to other people?

How often is the team celebrated?

What are the opportunities for the celebration?

In what ways are the small victories celebrated? What expressions could be used which could have a big impact?

In what ways are the great victories celebrated? What are the options before the decision?

How are other people included (relatives, friends, associates, collaborators, partners, clients, etc.) in the celebrations?

What are the times when each member of the team has the opportunity to be especially celebrated? In what way? How would you like to be celebrated?

What could be other specific reasons/occasions for celebration?

What related actions (awareness, promotion, donations, fundraising) can accompany the celebration in your specific context?

In what way is divinity involved?

10. CAPITAL AND RESOURCES

what are you working with?

What is the potential of the organization to create and multiply wealth?

What difference can resources make in an organization or business?

10.1. PERSPECTIVES THAT MAKE A DIFFERENCE

Does wealth create a rich mindset, or does a rich mindset create wealth?

Prosperity

Is prosperity an end in itself or a means?

What is the ultimate purpose of desired prosperity and resource acquisition?

[To what purpose might the one you thought of be subordinate?]

How sustainable is this? How unselfish is it?

What if the altruistic mentality was an essential key to true prosperity? What if it really is? How do you practice generosity?

Ownership And Management

What are the resources that are in your ownership?

What are the resources entrusted to you for administration and multiplication?

How do you relate differently to the two categories of resources?

What are the positive aspects of both categories?

Which of the two categories do you feel more responsible for managing?

What if the resources you own were entrusted to you for administration and multiplication?

What if this really is the actual reality, and the owner who entrusted it to you is the greatest and most respectable being in the universe?

Human Resources?

How are people different from other types of resources?

What is normal to do with all other types of resources, and is it atypical for people?

How would you feel If you were treated like an average resource?

What would be another more appropriate category in which you would fit he people who contribute to the mission of the organization, or business?

10.2. THE STRENGTHS OF THE ORGANIZATION

In addition to the identity elements (cap 6), which are your strengths?

What is your capital, begin with the intangible capital?

While many companies go bankrupt in the first year after having an optimistic start, what are the reasons why you will have a success story?

Accumulated Success

What are the most important achievements so far?

What is the public reputation so far?

How well known is your brand to the general public? What about the target one, the ideal one?

What is the satisfaction of those who benefit from the services or products offered?

How good are the relationships with other entities like: partners, employees, volunteers, suppliers, collaborators, authorities and state institutions?

What are the signals indicating the need for improvement? What aspects should be improved? What especially?

Current Capacity[33]

Currently, how big is your ability to create positive effects in the target area, in society and even externally?

What is your ability to manage your internal relations in a healthy way? What about external ones: suppliers, customers, partners, collaborators, institutions and authorities?

What is the team's ability to carry out their daily tasks and responsibilities?

What is your ability to meet your short-term goals and objectives?

In your current context, what is your ability to grow and develop in the next period?

What is your ability to efficiently manage time? What about finances? What about certain material resources?

What is your ability to solve possible internal problems, or prevent and overcome certain obstacles?

How could your common capacity increase? What specific capacity would stimulate also the growth of others?

What should happen to increase capacity? What exactly in the first place?

What risks do you take to increase your capacity?

What opportunities do you take advantage of?

What is the most appropriate strategy for increasing your capacity?

Potential Objective

What is your potential to constantly increase in performance, to aim towards higher achievements than the previous ones?

What is your potential for transformation? In what area or specific aspect?

Overall, what is the main quality or asset of the organization thanks to which you will write history? How could you be the best at this? What about the next quality or advantage?

How could you maximize your potential? How could you better highlight it? What is supposed to happen? What are you priorities?

10.3. MATERIAL RESOURCES

Beyond the strengths of the organization and the human contribution, what do you think are the most important resources needed to achieve the vision? How are they related to strategic objectives?

What are the company's most special resources?

What Are The Main Desired Investments?

How do you decide on what to invest?

The acquisition of which resources would be a great investment? For what period? With what impact? At what cost? How profitable?

Which resources have the greatest potential for long-term use? What is their long-term potential?

What is their market value?

What do you think the impact will be in the end?

How does this translate into numbers? What about reported at the cost of the investment?

How long is the investment amortized?

What is the value of the investment relative to the estimated lifespan? What about monthly or yearly?

What are the factors involved in making the investment?

How do you plan your investment?

How do you materialize it?

What Resources Do You Currently Need?

After what criteria do you purchase them?

Which should have the highest reliability?

Where does the quality matter most?

What else matters in purchases?

How could you find what you want at a competitive price?

How do you differentiate between what is indispensable, what is needed and different desires?

Finance

How do you create budgets?

For what purposes?

For what period?

What are your priorities? After what criteria?

What are your strategic goals? How many percent are investments?

What do you tend to neglect? How could you be more objective?

How sustainable is it? What are the risk elements?

How could you better estimate your expenses? What about income?

What are the fixed amounts and which are not?

What are the main categories of income?

What is the potential of each source of income?

What are the decisive moments for maximizing them?

What are the factors you need to take into account in the proper income forecasting, for the target period?

Management

How do you manage finances?

How do you make sure they are properly administered?

What system do you use? With what key elements?

Space Management

How satisfied are you with the location where you (want to) work?

How important is the workspace for you?

What are the positive aspects in the present situation?

In what ways could it be better? What should be changed for this to happen?

How could you make improvements in the area? What about facilities? What about the interior arrangement? What about aspects of comfort and decoration? What about the location? What about expanding to another location?

How can you streamline utility costs?

What are the criteria for obtaining the necessary materials? What are your quality standards?

What are the most used resources? What about the least used ones?

What are the resources you need to own and which could be rented? What are the resources you could change? How could you revaluate the old ones? What are the advantages for each type of procurement?

10.4. TIME MANAGEMENT

How do you know when you are near a turning point, of great importance? How could you be more involved in their definition?

What are the most time consuming factors?

How much time is given to priorities? On what should I spend more time?

Where could I save time?

Where could you make optimizations for more efficiency in using other resources over time? How could you maximize durability?

What is the farthest planned action?

What does the annual planning look like? What about the monthly one? What about the weekly one?

How are emergencies handled? How could this be prevented or better managed?

What are the activities whose importance is not reflected in the time allotted? Which are the main ones?

APPENDIX 1. CULTIVATING MULTIPLICATION

For growth and development, which of the following two ways do you want more: by adding or by multiplication? What are the advantages of long-term multiplication?

How would you describe a truly sustainable organization or business?

What favors a culture of multiplication? What is the prevailing attitude?

How does the ideal multiplication you dream of look like? What motivates you the most for it?

What are the reasons why some organizations and businesses fail to multiply?

What driving limits restraint multiplication?

What are other factors that prevent multiplication?

What are the implications in the absence of multiplication?

What are the temptations to reach a superficial multiplication?

What compromises would be counterproductive?

What are your principles for a sustainable multiplication?

How could it be more strategic? Or simpler? Or more efficient?

How could the rhythm of multiplication be increased?

How could the risks be diminished?

What would continue the multiplication?

> *In your current context, how do you imagine multiplication?*

> *What are your multiplication goals? What time interval?*

> *What aspects are essential for a healthy multiplication in your specific situation?*

> *What is limiting your multiplication at present?*

> *What changes should you make to better position yourself for multiplication?*

BIBLIOGRAPHY

1. The Four Lenses of Innovation: A Power Tool for Creative Thinking – Rowan Gibson
2. Type Talk at Work: How the 16 Personality Types That Determine Your Succes on The Job – Otto Kroeger with Jannet M. Thuesen & Hile Ruthledge
3. Type Talk: The 16 Personality Types That Determine How We Live, Love, and Work - Otto Kroeger and Jannet M. Thuesen
4. Culture of Honor – Danny Silk
5. Poverty, wealth, and wealth – Kris Vallatton
6. Visionary Leadership Skills, Creating a World to Which People Want to Belong – Robert B. Dilts
7. Leading like Jesus, 40 Leadership Lessons from the Upside-Down Kingdom – Floyd McClung
8. The Trusted Leader, 3 keys to becoming the kind of leader others want to follow – Terry Cook

- www.16personalities.com
- www.123test.com/disc-personality-test
- www.123test.com/what-is-disc/
- www.123test.com/disc-profiles/
- www.discprofiles.com/blog/2013/06/everything-disc-leadership-styles
- www.tests.enneagraminstitute.com
- www.lakenokomispc.org/up-

- loads/2/9/8/7/29872037/quest_pg_1_test.pdf
- www.damaideparte.ro/psihologie-practica/testul-eneagramei/
- www.theenneagraminbusiness.com/business-applications/leadership/

Notes:

[1] Concrete practice to the passage with the same title, from the *Visionary Mentality*, chapter 3

[2] Concrete practice to the passage with the same title, from the *Visionary Mentality*, chapter 3

[3] Concrete practice to the passage with the same title, from the *Visionary Mentality*, chapter 3

[4] Concrete applications to the same title section of the *Visionary mentality*, cap 3

[5] Concrete applications to the same title section of the *Visionary mentality*, cap 3

---

[1] The Four Lenses of Innovation: A Power Tool for Creative Thinking, Rowan Gibson, pg. 18-27

[2] https://www.16personalities.com/ - MBTI test

[3] Type Talk at Work: How the 16 Personality Types That Determine Your Succes on The Job - Otto Kroeger with Jannet Mr Thuesen - Hile Ruthledge, 2001 - Cape 6

[4] Type Talk at Work: How the 16 Personality Types That Determine Your Succes on The Job - Otto Kroeger with Jannet Mr Thuesen - Hile Ruthledge, 2001 - Cape 6

[5] Type Talk: The 16 Personality Types That Determine How We Live, Love, and Work Otto Kroeger - Jannet M. Thuesen, 1989 - pg. 53-55

[6] Type Talk: The 16 Personality Types That Determine How We Live, Love, and Work Otto Kroeger - Jannet M. Thuesen, 1989 - pg. 261-265

[7] Type Talk: The 16 Personality Types That Determine How We Live, Love, and Work Otto Kroeger - Jannet M. Thuesen, 1989 - pg. 276-280

[8] Type Talk: The 16 Personality Types That Determine How We Live, Love, and Work Otto Kroeger - Jannet M. Thuesen, 1989 - pg. 243 - 246

[9] Type Talk: The 16 Personality Types That Determine How We Live, Love, and Work Otto Kroeger - Jannet M. Thuesen, 1989 - pg. 226-229

[10] Type Talk: The 16 Personality Types That Determine How We Live, Love, and Work

BIBLIOGRAPHY

Otto Kroeger - Jannet M. Thuesen, 1989 - pg. 256-261

[11] Type Talk: The 16 Personality Types That Determine How We Live, Love, and Work Otto Kroeger - Jannet M. Thuesen, 1989 - pg. 272-276

[12] Type Talk: The 16 Personality Types That Determine How We Live, Love, and Work Otto Kroeger - Jannet M. Thuesen, 1989 - pg. 238-243

[13] Type Talk: The 16 Personality Types That Determine How We Live, Love, and Work Otto Kroeger - Jannet M. Thuesen, 1989 - pg. 222-226

[14] Type Talk: The 16 Personality Types That Determine How We Live, Love, and Work Otto Kroeger - Jannet M. Thuesen, 1989 - pg. 58-59

[15] Type Talk: The 16 Personality Types That Determine How We Live, Love, and Work Otto Kroeger - Jannet M. Thuesen, 1989 - pg. 55-56

[16] https://www.123test.com/disc-personality-test/ -DISK Test, June 27, 2019

[17] https://www.123test.com/what-is-disc/ -27 June 2019

[18] https://www.123test.com/disc-profiles/ -27 June 2019

[19] https://www.discprofiles.com/blog/2013/06/everything-disc-leadership-styles/ -27 June 2019

[20] https://tests.enneagraminstitute.com/ - Enneagram Test, 27 June 2019

[21] http://www.lakenokomispc.org/uploads/2/9/8/7/29872037/quest_pg_1_test.pdf - Quick Enneagram Sortins Test https://www.damaideparte.ro/psihologie-practica/testul-eneagramei/ -Version Romanian, 27 June 2019

[22] https://theenneagraminbusiness.com/business-applications/leadership/ - 28 Aug 2019

[23] Culture of Honor, Danny Silk, Destiny Image, 2009, pg. 117-146

[24] Sărăcie, Bogăție și Avuții, Kris Vallatton, Alfa Omega, 2018, pg. 121-132, 159-177

[25] The Four Lenses of Innovation: A Power Tool for Creative Thinking, Rowan Gibson, pg. 28-30, 57

[26] The Four Lenses of Innovation: A Power Tool for Creative Thinking, Rowan Gibson, pg. 31-35, 57

[27] The Four Lenses of Innovation: A Power Tool for Creative Thinking, Rowan Gibson, pg. 36-45, 57

[28] The Four Lenses of Innovation: A Power Tool for Creative Thinking, Rowan Gibson, pg. 46-55, 57

[29] Blanchard & Hersey conform cu: Visionary Leadership Skills, Creating a World to Which People Want to Belong, Robert B. Dilts, Cap 7, 1996

[30] Bass, conform cu Visionary Leadership Skills, Creating a World to Which People Want to Belong, Robert B. Dilts, Cap 7, 1996

[31] Leading like Jesus, 40 Leadership Lessons from the Upside-Down Kingdom, Floyd

McClung, Lesson 30

[32] The Trusted Leader, 3 kEys to becoming the kind of leader others want to follow, Terry Cook, pg 7

[33] Sărăcie, Bogăție și Avuții, Kris Vallatton, Alfa Omega, 2018, pg. 143-157

ABOUT THE AUTHOR

Mihail Bogdan

Husband for Ema, best friend and colleague: first in the staff team, then in the leadership team, then in the pioneering team and now in the new leadership team.

Father to Timotei and Sara, my children who overwhelm me with their unconditional love and continuous development.

Pioneer, leader and teacher in probably the most diverse and dynamic movement with global impact, YWAM.

Spirituality blogger about at www.nouacreatie.ro
Leadership Coaching at visionarycoaching.eu

Life Coach passionate to inspire and empower new leaders for pioneering, development and multiplication.

Printed in Great Britain
by Amazon